HELP!!!

I HAVE A PROPERTY INSURANCE CLAIM

KARL HECHAVARRIA
AIC, FCIP, CRM, CFE, RPA, ACA

Previously published as:
How to Negotiate Higher Insurance Claims Settlements

Order this book online at www.trafford.com
or email orders@trafford.com

Most Trafford titles are also available at major online book retailers.

Note for Librarians: A cataloguing record for this book is available from Library
and Archives Canada at www.collectionscanada.ca/amicus/index-e.html

Printed in Victoria, BC, Canada.

ISBN: 978-1-4251-7209-1

*Our mission is to efficiently provide the world's finest, most comprehensive book publishing
service, enabling every author to experience success. To find out how to publish your
book, your way, and have it available worldwide, visit us online at www.trafford.com*

Trafford rev. 8/13/2009

 www.trafford.com

North America & international
toll-free: 1 888 232 4444 (USA & Canada)
phone: 250 383 6864 ♦ fax: 812 355 4082

INTRODUCTION

This book covers the most common types of wording found in homeowners, condominium and tenants insurance policies. Some companies offer exotic types of coverage which is so unusual that it would not be applicable to the average reader of this book.

It is known that six of every ten insureds will have at least one homeowner's claim during their lifetime. Some claims will be due to carelessness or negligent acts, but most will be weather related.

The purpose of this book is to provide general guidelines for the policy holder in understanding the policy provisions and the claims adjustment procedures. It does not cover complex or legal issues. Accounting, legal or other experts should be retained in those circumstances by the policy holder.

The author or publisher assume no liability or obligation associated with any loss or risk which might result directly or indirectly from the information contained in this book.

CONTENTS

CHAPTER 1
The Application

There are two methods used by insurance companies to sell their policies. One sells directly to the public through agents who are salaried employees of the company and may also receive a commission based on sales. These companies are known as direct writers. Other companies sell through agents or brokers who are independent business owners and are paid a commission based on sales. These companies are indirect writers. Agents or brokers usually sell policies for more than one insurance company, although it is possible for them to sell exclusively for one company. Some companies utilize both distribution methods.

During your initial contact with the sales person, the application form is completed. This gives the company the information needed to determine the amount of insurance that is adequate and the premium, which is the cost of the policy.

The application is divided into sections. It covers the following:
- Personal information – name, address and other basics
- Type of construction – frame, brick, brick veneer, concrete block
- Size – square footage, number of stories
- Occupancy – owner occupied, rental, including home based business
- Building valuation – the amount to replace the building
- Additional liability exposures – swimming pool, animals
- Optional coverage – replacement cost or actual cash value.

A very important part of the application is the section dealing with prior claims. That section explores the applicant's claims history over the years. Some companies want a claims history of two years, others as much as five. It is very important that the applicant is truthful when answering this question. Firstly, the company takes into account the claims history of the applicant among other factors in calculating the premium. Secondly, if it is later determined that the applicant did not disclose prior claims history or relevant negative information about the property, any future claim may be denied based on misrepresentation. In other words, the company can take the position that had the underwriter known all the facts about the property or prior claims, they would not have accepted the applicant as an insured. Sometimes, if every negative factor is disclosed, the applicant may still be acceptable but at a higher premium. If an application was accepted based on a misrepresentation (false or withheld information), and while investigating a subsequent claim, the prior claims history or the true condition of the property is discovered, the company may void the policy '*ab initio*' (which means 'from the beginning'). The company would refund the premium and deny the claim regardless of the amount or severity. Alternatively, at their option, the company may elect to retroactively charge the insured the additional premium that should have been collected when the policy was first issued, and honor the current claim as presented.

The courts have upheld the insurers' position that a policy is written based on 'utmost good faith' by both parties. It is assumed that the information provided by the applicant is correct, and if it is not, the insurer has been prejudiced by accepting the applicant without knowing all the facts. Each company sets the number of prior claims within a specified period that's acceptable. It may be five claims within the past four years or three within two years or whatever number the company deems as an acceptable level.

An insurance company does not send an inspector to your home to check on the accuracy of the information prior to accepting the risk. Some companies will ask the agent/broker to send a photo of the exterior of the house to be insured. This is not the normal practice in Canada, but is usually required in the United States. There are some insurers that specialize in insuring high valued homes or estates as they are sometimes called. These insurers will send an appraiser to the home to determine the value of the contents prior to, or shortly after issuing the policy. This will be covered more extensively in Chapter 6.

Equally important on the application are questions dealing with prior cancellation, declination or refusal to renew your insurance by your previous insurer. This implies to the prospective insurer that there may have been a problem with your former insurance company, or problems in trying to get coverage. The prospective insurer will check with your prior insurer to determine the reason for the non renewal, and decide if they want to accept you as an insured. Some brokers may, and should ask questions about any prior insurance problems during the course of completing your application. This is a good business practice by the agent as it allows him to plead your case with the underwriter if he has to overcome the underwriter's reluctance to accept your application. This also saves the agent time as he knows his market (i.e. – the companies with whom he places business), and will allow him to place your application with a company most likely to accept you as an insured. This avoids having to approach numerous companies in order to place your business since he also knows the underwriting rules of the companies with whom he places his clients. Brokers know the concept of utmost good faith and will ask detailed questions in order to qualify you for insurance.

Another important question relates to business pursuits done in the home. Withholding information regarding certain activities may result in future claims being denied due to coverage issues. Companies allow some home based business pursuits, but there are exceptions. For example, most companies will not insure a home where there are paid full time baby sitting services. Occasional baby sitting for a friend with or without payment might be acceptable to the company. On the other hand, paid professional day care exposes the company to risks they may not be willing to underwrite. Recent court cases have found insureds liable if a minor has been sexually molested while in their care or have been exposed to harm or illness due to negligence. Companies may not want to insure a home where the home based business results in heavy pedestrian traffic which exposes the company to trip and fall injury claims.

There have been cases where hosts have been found negligent by providing alcohol to a guest, who while driving home impaired, has an accident resulting in an injury or fatality to himself or an innocent victim. These types of host liquor liability cases are getting more frequent. Insurers are also becoming increasingly reluctant to underwrite homes where there are other types of business endeavors which create unacceptable exposures. Chapter 8 explores this issue more closely.

The occupancy of the home is also of importance. If there is a claim involving roomers or boarders, insurers may take the position that the application states they were insuring a family occupied home, and had they known about the rental arrangement, would not have accepted the risk. Applicants should disclose if any portion of the house is rented to others to avoid potential problems if a claim is made.

Questions relating to the type of heating, distance from a fire hydrant and the age of the home are detailed in the application. If the home is heated with a wood burning stove, that is an important underwriting factor which may affect acceptance of the application or the premium to be charged. Wood stoves can cause fires if they were improperly installed.

Similarly, a house located far from a fire station or a fire hydrant creates a greater exposure and may result in a total loss fire. To a lesser extent, so are locations that are dependent on a volunteer fire department which may not be as well trained or efficient as a fire department in a large city staffed by professional fire fighters.

The condition of the plumbing, heating, electrical wiring, roofing and the general condition of a house are directly related to the age of the house unless replacement or upgrading has been done since it was built. Building ordinances (or codes) are in place in all states and provinces. Aluminum wiring may no longer conform to the building ordinance. To repair the structure following a loss may involve upgrading to satisfy the new building codes. Court decisions on this topic will be reviewed in later chapters.

The broker will calculate the amount of coverage needed. This is done by using a replacement cost calculator common in the industry. Using the square footage of the house, the number of stories, type of construction, number of bathrooms and other additional features or upgrades, the agent can calculate the replacement cost. Some insurers require a surcharge if the home is over a certain age, usually if more than twenty five years.

Some homeowners think that if their house has a market value of $200,000, that is the correct amount of insurance that should be purchased in order to rebuild the structure in case of a total loss. You must remember that the value of the land is included in the market value. That may be the correct selling price or market value, but even if the home was completely destroyed, the land itself is undamaged, consequently the land value should not be included in the amount of insurance needed.

In addition, if the house has a basement, it is unlikely that the basement walls would be damaged to the extent that a complete replacement would be necessary. That should also be taken into account when deciding the amount of insurance needed. Discuss these points with your broker when applying for insurance.

If you are a tenant or a condominium unit owner, the application is less comprehensive. The reason is that you are only insuring limited building coverage, your household contents, liability exposure and other added basic coverage. Chapter 2 has more details on this point.

A condominium unit owner's policy does not insure the building. Two separate policies are in effect. The Master Policy covers the building structure and common areas, while the unit owner's policy provides coverage for contents, improvements and betterments and personal liability. The condominium board of directors is responsible to secure insurance for the building.

The main coverage additions are the unit owner's betterments and improvements and assessments. If a loss is covered by both the master and the unit owner's policies, the master policy pays first (becoming the primary payer). Please refer to Chapter 2 for details.

An important issue regarding the application is the obligations of your broker. Remember that an 'agent' or 'broker' means basically the same when referring to individuals licensed to sell insurance to the public. Throughout this book, reference will be made to an agent or broker interchangeably. Some states and provinces have changed their Insurance Act to clearly define the legal status of each. This was as a result of law suits involving insurance sales personnel who were alleged to have acted against the best interest of either their client (the insurance buyer) or the insurance company whose policies they were selling.

The question faced by the courts was whether the agent was acting as an agent of the insured or the insurer. The answer to that question impacted on the courts' decisions. By ensuring that all insurance sales staff are called brokers, some states and provinces made it clear by definition that sellers are in fact working in the best interest of the insurance buyer. In effect, they are working for the insured as they sought to get the best price and coverage for the insured, even if a broker or agent signs a contract with more than one insurance company to sell their policies. The seller is given binding authority which means that once the application is completed, he can immediately tell his client that the house is insured for the amount requested. The insurance company is then bound to honor the terms of the contract. If the company later discovers that the information on the application was incorrect because the broker deliberately changed the answers given by the applicant in order to get acceptance by the insurer, or if the broker 'bound' (accepted on behalf of the insurer) a risk he was not authorized to bind under his contract with the insurer, the insurance company has options depending on the circumstances.

If the inaccurate information is discovered while investigating a subsequent claim, the insurer may be forced to pay the claim, if the insured was unaware that the broker changed the information he was given when the application was being completed. The insurer would seek reimbursement from the broker. The broker would most likely involve his 'Errors and Omissions' insurance policy, which usually responds in those situations. This type of policy is sold to various professionals and is frequently referred to as an 'E & O' policy. It covers negligent acts by professionals. The key word is negligent. If the broker's actions are such that it could be regarded as fraudulent as opposed to carelessness or an oversight, the E & O policy would not provide coverage as insurance policies do not cover criminal or fraudulent acts. If the insured was not paid by his own insurer or by the broker's E & O insurer, the broker would be personally responsible to pay the insured. If the insurer paid the claim, the broker would reimburse the insurer.

On the other hand, if the misinformation on the application was discovered before a claim was made against the policy, the insurer would seek to clarify the information or simply cancel the policy as required under the State or Provincial Insurance Act.

The normal requirement is that a registered letter of cancellation is sent to the insured's last known address, and that proof that the letter was sent is kept by the insurer. Most companies routinely prepare a list of registered letters mailed on a daily basis, and that list is accepted as proof by the court that the cancellation letter was sent.

If the letter is returned because the insured moved, or refuses delivery, the insurance company will keep the returned letter (unopened) with the notation written on the envelope by the post office giving the reason why they were unable to deliver the letter. If the insurer received the premium with the application from the broker, they must return the premium less the appropriate deduction for short term cancellation. This means the insurer will keep a portion of the premium for the time they provided coverage, plus a processing fee. The amount kept is not proportionate for the time on risk. For example, let's assume a premium of $120 for one year's coverage. If the policy is cancelled two months later, you would not get a refund of $100, which is $120 divided by 12 (to get the monthly premium), less two months coverage. The cost for the additional paperwork is passed on to the insured.

The cancellation notice will have a date on which coverage will cease. This will give you time to insure with another company, usually using the same broker, unless you decide otherwise. If the insurer is tardy in returning the unearned premium, (that portion of the premium that has not been used because of the short time the insurer provided coverage), it could be argued that coverage is still in effect despite the cancellation letter. In some cases, the courts have ruled that the unearned premium must be returned with the cancellation letter to terminate coverage on the date stated in the letter. Until the insured receives the unearned premium, coverage is still in effect and any claim presented within that period must be paid, regardless of the cancellation date stated in the letter.

CHAPTER 2
Types of Policies

This chapter addresses the most common homeowner, condominium and tenant policies written in the United States and the three most common policies written in Canada. A summary of these policies are as follows.

Homeowners Policy – Basic Form HO-1

This form is rarely offered by insurers over the past few years. It provides named perils coverage on Dwelling, Other Structures and Personal Property. 'Named Perils' mean that the policy will cover loss or damage to the building structure or other structures located within your property line, and your household contents if the loss or damage is caused by a named peril (which is the cause of loss – fire, windstorm etc). The policy specifically lists the perils which would activate coverage. If the loss is caused by any peril not listed in the policy, there is no coverage. The appeal for this type of limited coverage is the price since it is the cheapest on the market. In Canada, this policy is known as a 'Standard Homeowners' policy.

Homeowners Policy – Broad Form HO-2

The main difference between the coverage offered by the HO-1 and HO-2 forms is that the HO-2 form provides broad protection for your dwelling, other structures and contents. 'Broad Form' coverage means that in addition to the perils named in the HO-1 form, the HO-2 has additional perils which are covered. In Canada, the Broad Form coverage is unlike the HO-2 form. It is comparable to the HO-3 Special form.

Homeowners Policy – Special Form HO-3

This type of policy provides 'All Risk' (sometimes called 'All Peril') coverage except when certain types of losses to the dwelling, personal property and other structures are excluded. Although it suggests that every loss would be covered, there are no policies that will pay for every cause of loss. To offer unlimited coverage would result in premiums which would be so expensive, it would be unaffordable for the average consumer. In addition, such a policy would pay for maintenance, such as repairs needed because of normal wear and tear or weathering over the years. Insurance covers sudden and accidental losses. Consequently, there are exclusions which would preclude coverage for certain losses and normal deterioration that takes place slowly over a long period of time.

Contents or personal property are covered under 'Named Perils' as previously mentioned. To refresh the reader's memory, this means the policy specifically lists the causes of loss that are covered.

Special Personal Property – HO-15
In the United States, for an additional premium, an insured can purchase this coverage. This form is used in conjunction with the HO-3 policy and provides coverage for additional perils for dwelling, other structures and contents that is not included in the standard HO-3. This additional coverage form lists losses that are specifically excluded. To cite one example, it covers loss by wind as opposed to windstorm. The HO-3 covers windstorm but not wind. Wind coverage pays for damages caused by wind gusts even if it is not classified as a storm, tornado or hurricane by the national weather service.

Homeowners Policy – Contents Broad Form HO-4
Although this form is called a 'Homeowners Policy,' it is only sold to tenants. There is no coverage for the dwelling structure or other structures except under the liability section of the policy in the event a loss was caused by the negligence of the tenant. This aspect of coverage is discussed in Chapter 8. This form provides Broad Form coverage on a named peril basis (causes of loss are listed) for loss or damage to the tenant's (who is the insured) personal property.

In Canada, this type of policy is called a 'Standard Tenants Package.' In both the United States and Canada however, many companies are now offering all peril coverage, subject to the standard exclusions, to tenants who want broader coverage.

Condominium Unit Owners Form -- HO-6

Some states enacted a law that requires every condominium unit owner to carry hazard and liability insurance even if there is no mortgage on the property. The reason for this requirement is to protect other unit owners from a loss (fire, water damage etc.) caused by a negligent unit owner. A Condominium Unit owners' policy provides a broader coverage than a tenant's policy. The tenant's policy covers the personal property of the tenant. The Condominium policy offers limited building coverage over and above the master policy which covers the building. This may include appliances, counter tops and other similar types of property which is your responsibility to insure under the Condominium Corporation, Association of Property Owner's agreement or Home Owners Associations. Coverage is also extended to other structures owned exclusively by you at the location of the residence premises. It also offers additional coverage for improvements and betterments. For example, the owner may have upgraded the unit when the purchase was made. The increased cost is regarded as betterment (at time of purchase) or improvement (done subsequently). The point that you must remember is that if the unit was purchased with wall to wall carpeting and wallpaper without an additional cost to the insured, those items are considered as a part of the building and is covered by the building's master policy. If at the time of purchase, the insured paid an additional amount for carpeting and wallpaper, it would be considered as betterment. If it was done after the purchase, it would be an improvement. Those items would then be covered under the unit owner's policy since the insured paid for them separately. The upgrades are an additional expense, and give the owner a financial interest over and above the basic purchase price of the unit. The policy protects the owner against the additional costs to repair or replace the betterments or improvements. Let's review a mixed situation. The owner purchased the unit with the carpets and wallpaper valued at $5,000 which was included in the purchase price. He upgraded the carpets and wallpaper and paid an additional $3,000. Following a loss, the master policy covering the building would pay up to $5,000 towards replacing the upgraded carpets and wallpaper, and the unit owner's policy would pay the additional $3,000. The rule of thumb is that the building master policy pays to repair the unit to the original condition at the time of purchase. The Condominium Unit Owners policy would pay the additional costs, if any, to replace/repair the upgraded items.

A unique feature of the Condominium policy is the Loss Assessment insuring clause. This allows the policy to pay up to a stated amount, usually $1,000, (or it could be increased to $2,000) if as a unit owner, you are assessed an amount by the condominium corporation for a loss as a result of a peril that is also insured by your unit owner's policy. It does not pay however, for any assessment by a government department or for damage caused by a peril excluded in your policy. For example, if a hurricane damages the roof of the building and the master policy's limit is insufficient to complete repairs or replacement, the condo board would assess an amount to be paid by each unit owner to make up the shortfall. Since the unit owner's policy also covers hurricane damage, the assessment section of the policy would respond. If however, the roof was being repaired or replaced due to age and wear and tear, it would be a maintenance issue and the policy would not pay the assessed amount. Both the Canadian and U.S. policies provide the same condominium coverage.

Homeowners Policy – Modified Coverage Form HO-8
This insurance contract is similar to HO-1, except that some of the coverage is limited. This policy is targeted to areas not considered desirable from an insurance standpoint. This form is not available in Canada. Special sub-limits are reduced, and perils are operative on a restricted basis. Insureds with this type of policy should familiarize themselves with the various restrictions. The purpose of this book is to give a cursory overview of the differences between the policies offered by various companies to protect the homeowner, condo unit owner or renter from a loss.

In some states, there are laws that allow communities to form Home Owners Associations referred to as HOA's. There are covenants which allow HOA's to enforce the rules of the communities, and if necessary impose an assessment against each homeowner similar to a condominium board. Because of the growing numbers of HOA's, insurers are providing assessment coverage in some of their homeowner's policies. The coverage is activated in the same manner as in the condominium policies.

Fines imposed by the HOA are not covered by any policy. If a homeowner is fined for violating any of the rules and regulations of the HOA, payment is the sole responsibility of the homeowner.

In the United States, insurers offer Homeowners and Dwelling policies for buildings not exceeding four units (apartments). Buildings with more than four units must get a commercial property policy. In order for a four unit building to qualify for a homeowner's policy, the insured (owner) must reside in one of the units at the residence.

The 'Dwelling Program' offers three types of policies. Dwelling Program policies are not offered in Canada as Canadian homeowner's policies are customized to cover rental premises with appropriate exclusions. In the United States, dwelling policies are available in three separate forms. They are Basic DP-1, Broad DP-2 and Special DP-3 forms.

DP-1 and DP-2 provide dwelling (building) coverage and contents on an actual cash value basis while the DP-3 provides all peril coverage on the building. All 3 policies provide coverage for other detached structures within the property line based on 10% of the dwelling limit. Contents located in the rented unit(s) owned by the insured (not the tenant – eg: refrigerator, stove, built in dishwasher etc), are covered on an actual cash value basis. Coverage is also provided for 'Fair Rental Value' if the tenant(s) move out due to damage to the building caused by a covered peril, until the repairs are completed. The insured would be able to collect rent as if the building was still occupied and also additional living expenses for

13

himself if he normally resided in the building and also had to temporarily relocate while the damages were being repaired. Additional living expenses must be added by endorsement to the DP-1 policy. Losses covered by DP-1 are fire, lightening and internal explosion (within the premises). Additional coverage can be added by endorsement and paying the additional premium.

The Broad form (DP-2) covers the 3 causes of loss provided by the DP-1 and adds 8 other covered perils.

The Special form (DP-3) provides the same coverage as the DP-2, but in addition, it provides all risk coverage on the building subject to exclusions. Some insurers offer coverage that may be different from what is stated in this section. It is recommended that you review your policy carefully.

Mobile or Motor Home policies are not reviewed in this chapter. A brief overview regarding the adjusting process can be found in Chapter 9.

CHAPTER 3
Classification of Adjusters

There are three types of adjusters: staff, independent and public.

Staff adjusters are employees of the insurance company's claims department. They are also called claims representatives. Within that group, they are broken down into field (road adjusters), office (inside or telephone adjusters) and some companies have claims clerks who handle 'bill payer' type claims. Bill payer claims are claims made by insureds that require no investigation, and once coverage is confirmed, the claims are paid based on replacement/repair receipts or invoices. Staff adjusters are paid a salary and do not get a commission or bonus based on money saved when the adjustment process is completed. Some insureds believe that when a payment is less than the amount claimed, the adjuster gets a commission or bonus. This is illegal and would result in serious consequences by the regulators should an insurer indulge in such practices. Some jurisdictions require that staff adjusters must be licensed by the state or province.

The training given to staff adjusters varies. Some insurance companies have elaborate and sophisticated training facilities and courses, while others use independent schools offering claims adjusting courses. Some of these schools or community colleges are allowed to administer state licensing tests at the conclusion of the course. There are companies which do neither, and the training is done on the job. This type of training involves the adjusting of small first party claims and assuming greater responsibilities as their experience level increases. Some field adjusters are trained to prepare repair estimates, while some companies will rely on estimates provided by independent contractors retained by the company or the insured. Some adjusters are multi-line trained. This means they are proficient in adjusting automobile, property or liability claims. Some adjusters are specialist and adjust only one type of claim. This specialization could be in auto, property, commercial, liability, bond, freight or other types of claims requiring special training and experience. Having the specialist designation however, does not guarantee that the individual has in fact been trained to the level of an expert in that field. It could simply mean that the adjuster handles only one type of claim because of the size or structure of the company's claims department.

Field adjusters usually handle large or complex losses, and/or investigate fraud cases. The adjuster's investigation is done at the loss site to ensure that the adjustment procedure is well documented via statements, photographs or video, relevant documents and conducts any necessary interviews needed to successfully conclude the loss, or deny payment if the investigation led to that decision.

In the late 1970's, insurance companies realized that they had to find a more efficient and economical way to adjust medium size losses. This resulted in a second category of adjusters known as office or telephone adjusters. These staff adjusters handle losses via the telephone. If it is necessary to obtain a formal statement, they are trained to obtain a recorded statement over the telephone. The recording can be transcribed, and if necessary mailed to the individual who consented to the recording for a signature. This has the same effect as obtaining a signed statement without the expense of involving a field adjuster. The taking of a recorded statement is legal provided the person being recorded gives their consent. To avoid being accused of obtaining the recording without the person's consent, the consent and knowledge that the party is aware that the conversation is being recorded is included on the tape at both the beginning and again at the end.

Some claims clerks are allowed to adjust bill payer type claims. These claims usually involve glass breakage, theft of one or more inexpensive items and do not involve liability decisions. If during the information gathering phase fraud is suspected, the file is transferred to a more experienced adjuster or the Special Investigation Unit (SIU).

Special Investigation Units are comprised of staff adjusters trained to investigate suspicious claims or staff investigators with a law enforcement or fire investigation background. Staff adjusters in an SIU can quantify and pay claims if their investigation determines that there was no fraud attempt. On the other hand, ex police officers or fire investigators in the SIU do not adjust claims. Once their investigation is complete, the file is given to an adjuster for payment or a formal denial, and is handled by the adjuster to conclusion.

Independent Adjusters are independent claims professionals that are licensed by the state or province to adjust claims, and can only do so if they are hired by an insurance company. They must be licensed by passing either a written and/or oral exam. They adjust claims on a fee for service basis and are hired by insurance companies that do not have a claims staff. The insurance companies have on staff claims examiners who review the independent adjusters' reports. Sometimes independent adjusters are hired because the company needs their special expertise in adjusting certain types of claims which may not be available within the company's claims department. In most cases the company, when faced with an unusually heavy volume of claims hire independent adjusters for assistance. This may occur after a hurricane, tornado, ice storm, earthquake, hailstorm or any other catastrophic situation. Claims must be dealt with quickly to speed up the repair process and to minimize additional damage. Independent adjusters charge a flat fee per claim or an hourly rate plus expenses. These fees are paid by the insurance company. Some states and provinces require continuing education to renew their licenses. Once the adjuster leaves the jurisdiction in which the license was granted, the license is no longer valid.

Independent adjusting firms vary in size. They range from a sole proprietor operation to national or international corporations with thousands of employees and offices located around the world. If an independent adjusting firm is retained, it does not mean that the claim will be adjusted by a licensed adjuster. Each state or province has different regulations and some allow licensing levels.

A junior in an office may be level one, and over the years, will pass progressively more technical exams until fully licensed. If a claim is adjusted by an unlicensed trainee, the file must be reviewed by a fully licensed staff member of the firm to ensure that proper adjusting procedures were followed. In some jurisdictions, before the trainee's reports are sent to the insurance company, they must be signed by a fully licensed member of the independent adjusting firm.

As stated earlier it is not unusual for an insurer to retain an independent adjusting firm after a catastrophe generating a large volume of claims. In order to settle claims quickly, some insurers may give the firm or the independent adjuster a monetary settlement authority. That authority level allows the independent adjuster to commit the insurer to pay the claim up to the dollar authority given by the insurer. Coverage issues must be submitted to the insurer for a decision and the adjuster can make no commitment on coverage to the insured regardless of the amount being claimed. Rarely will insurers give checks to independent adjusters to pay claims because of the potential check signature issues with the insurer's bank. If the claim exceeds the adjuster's monetary authority, he cannot commit the insurer to the payment without the insurers claims examiner's approval.

Independent adjusters have no authority to commit an insurer to a payment except in a catastrophic situation described above. After investigating a claim, he makes recommendations to his principals (the insurance company), and await their decision. The company is not obliged to accept or act on the independent adjuster's recommendation unless there is an agreement regarding coverage and/or the amount to be paid. That is the primary reason why the independent adjuster cannot bind the insurer to a course of action. To do so would be acting beyond the scope of authority given to independent adjusters. Depending on the circumstances, an insurer may have to honor the claim based on the independent adjuster's commitment to the insured if he created an 'estoppel.' This means that the insured took certain actions based on the commitment by the independent adjuster that payment would be forthcoming from the insurance company.

The insured must be able to prove conclusively that the independent adjuster made the payment commitment and that he took certain actions based on the commitment. For example, an insured reported the theft of a mink coat that costs $15,000. The claim was assigned to an independent adjuster to be investigated. After obtaining statements, a police report and other proof of ownership documents, the adjuster told the insured that the claim will be paid in full. After reviewing the adjuster's report, the insurer's claims examiner discovered that the coat was not 'scheduled,' (meaning insured for the full replacement cost – see Chapter 6) and consequently, payment would be limited to the policy's maximum sub-limit for furs of $2,000. In the interim, the insured purchased another coat expecting to be fully reimbursed by her company. When told that the limit for the fur coat is $2,000, the insured demands payment in full. Her position was that the adjuster created an estoppel by his commitment that she would receive the full replacement cost, and that the company cannot after the fact invoke a coverage issue. The insured further stated that had she known the maximum payable was $2,000, she would either have accepted the $2,000 and not replaced the coat, or purchased a much cheaper one. Given those circumstances, the insurer would have to pay the full amount of $15,000 because the independent adjuster had created an estoppel.

All the ingredients for an estoppel are present in the above example. The independent adjuster is an agent of the insurer. Although he acted beyond the scope of his authority by committing the company to pay the full replacement cost and not the correct sub-limit, the insured had no reason to believe that her claim would not be paid in full and incurred an expense (replacement) based on that understanding. In addition, the insured had no obligation to question the authority of the independent adjuster. In that situation, the insurance company would pay the claim and decide if it should recover the difference of $13,000 from the independent adjuster. If the company insisted on reimbursement, the adjuster must either reimburse the insurer personally, or involve his Errors and Omissions insurer. They would conduct their own investigation and arrive at their own conclusion regarding the estoppel. However, if the insurer's claims examiner discovered the independent adjuster's error and informed the insured via a phone call and/or letter before she made the purchase and she did so anyway, there is no estoppel and the insurer would not be obligated to pay the full replacement cost.

This example is a simplified illustration of an estoppel. A staff adjuster under similar circumstances would also create an estoppel. If the staff adjuster proceeded to make the same commitment as the independent adjuster before confirming that the coat was scheduled, the company would be estopped by his actions.

The last category is Public Adjusters. Unlike staff or independent adjusters, the public adjuster works for the insured. Much like the independent adjuster, he must be licensed by the state or province and the licensing procedure is similar. In some jurisdictions, public adjusters are not allowed to represent an insured that has suffered a personal injury, and they are authorized to represent insureds in non injury losses only. A telephone call to the Department of Insurance or Financial Services should clarify the authority of public adjusters in your area, and can also confirm their license status. Their license are also subject to renewal and is not valid if they leave the jurisdiction in which the license was issued. Unlike the independent adjuster who is paid by the insurance company, the public adjuster signs a contract with the insured which obligates the insured to pay the public adjuster a percentage of the settlement. The average is between 5% and 10%. Some jurisdictions limit the percentage that the public adjuster can charge. The public adjuster acts on the insured's behalf in negotiating a settlement with the insurer. He obtains his own estimates, expert reports, relevant documents and negotiates directly with the insurance company's adjuster or the independent adjuster retained by the insurance company. He may also be involved in the arbitration or appraisal process if the claim can't be resolved by negotiation (see Chapter 4). If the parties fail to negotiate a settlement, the public adjuster would assist the attorney retained by the insured. A public adjuster offers his services to an insured by direct solicitation, or the insured will contact the public adjuster if he requires his assistance in preparing the claim to be presented to the insurer or if a settlement can't be reached with the insurer. The involvement of public adjusters in property losses is getting more prevalent as the public is becoming more aware of their existence. In order to ensure payment after the loss is settled, when the public adjuster is retained, he sends a written notice advising the insurer that he represents the insured. The insurer is obligated to include the public adjuster's name or firm on the settlement check.

When difficulties arise in the adjustment of a loss, it is not unusual for an insured to retain the services of an attorney to resolve the impasse. Immediately, a cost may be incurred as the attorney may request a retainer, or a consultation fee. Some attorneys will accept a case on a contingent fee basis. This means that the insured would pay nothing if the case was lost, or an agreed percentage of the settlement if successful. In some jurisdictions in Canada, contingent fee agreements are illegal. An attorney may be reluctant to enter into a contingent fee agreement when the claim involves a property loss. A personal injury case is more conducive to a contingent fee arrangement as the injured party is more than likely to get a monetary settlement. The outcome of a property loss in which quantum (the amount to be paid), or a coverage issue has a less certain result.

This chapter concludes with a brief overview of 'Bad Faith' claims against an insurer. The actions of an adjuster or insurer can result in an insured or claimant alleging bad faith. When an insurer is investigating a loss, it must be done in a fair, impartial and balanced manner without preconceptions as to the outcome. The *Unfair Claims Practices Act* dictates that adjusters investigate claims in a prompt impartial manner, and that a fair settlement offer must be made within a reasonable time frame. In addition, the settlement amount must be reasonable and is not to the detriment of the claimant or insured. An insured, claimant or both can bring an action alleging bad faith. Bad faith allegations are usually included in the 'Complaint' (a document filed with the court outlining the grounds for the lawsuit). In Canada, this document is called a 'Statement of Claim.' An allegation of bad faith can be made at any time during the negotiation phase of a claim. It can be added by amending the complaint or statement of claim to include the allegation of bad faith after the documents have been filed in the court. If the court finds that there were any serious impropriety in the handling of the claim, it can award the plaintiff (the person suing) an additional amount over and above the value of the claim to deter the insurer and the insurance industry in general from such dishonest or unethical activity in the future. The additional amount awarded is called punitive or exemplary damages.

CHAPTER 4
Policy Sections

This chapter is a review of the policy sections that provide the protection for the homeowner or tenant in the insurance contract.

Until the mid seventies, the contract wording of property insurance policies was confusing to the public who had difficulty determining coverage. The public was never certain that the adjuster was interpreting the insuring clauses or exclusions correctly. This led to numerous complaints to the regulatory bodies in the United States and Canada. Realizing the negative impact this had on the image and credibility of the industry, insurance companies decided to introduce a new version of the contract that was written in layman's terms and easily understood. This was called the 'Easy Read' versions which immediately gained acceptability by the public. It stated in clear language the duties of each party to the contract. It utilized simple definitions such as 'you (the insured) shall…' and 'we (the insurer) will…' All companies currently have their own versions of the revised policies on the market.

It should be noted that unlike the automobile policy, the insuring clauses are not mandated by statute. The legislators of each state or province dictate by law the basic coverage that must be included in the automobile policy. That is to ensure that every automobile policy provides a minimum basic coverage to compensate an innocent party who suffers injury due to the negligence of the driver of a vehicle. Insurance companies can provide additional coverage in the automobile contract to get an edge on their competitors. They can for example, offer lower deductibles for the same premium, or pay for replacement locks when an insured has car keys stolen or accident forgiveness among other benefits. They can enhance coverage, but cannot remove mandatory legislated coverage.

There are some statutory requirements that must be included in the wording of the homeowner/tenant/condominium policies. Unlike the automobile policies, the statutory conditions form only a small section of the property policies. Consequently, insurers can offer any type of coverage the consumer wants, or will buy if the price is reasonable. It is the marketplace, price and claims cost that prevents insurers from offering their products at a very low cost or a variety of exotic coverage which their competitors may not have. Excessive or exotic coverage could generate a large number of claims and consequently increase payments and lower profits. The reader must bear in mind that an insurance company is in the business of making money for their investors. It is not a non-profit or charitable organization.

The homeowner/tenant contracts consist of the following:

The Declaration Page
Insuring Agreement
Definitions

SECTION ONE – PROPERTY COVERAGE
Coverage A – Dwelling
Coverage B – Other Structures
Coverage C – Personal Property
Coverage D – Loss of Use
Additional Coverage
Perils Insured Against
Exclusions
Conditions

SECTION TWO – LIABILITY COVERAGE
Exclusions
Coverage E – Personal Liability
Coverage F – Medical Payments to Others
Additional Coverage
Conditions – SECTIONS ONE and TWO

As you review the policy, you will note that there is a 'Statutory Conditions' section. Policies issued in some states do not have that section, while in Canada all provinces require that it is included in all property policies. Statutory Conditions are detailed further in the appropriate section of this chapter.

The Declaration Page

This is called the coverage sheet or the 'Dec Page.' It shows the effective and expiration dates of the policy which is the policy term. It also shows basic information such as the policy number, type of policy, name and address of the insured, the address of the property insured which may be different if the property is a rented premises at a separate location, mortgagee(s), policy limits for the building, other structures (sometimes shown as detached or appurtenant structures), personal property (contents), loss or use (which is additional living expenses and fair rental value), limits of liability, medical payments, any applicable discounts and the premium. It gives a snapshot of the insured, the property and the coverage in force.

If you are on a budget plan, it may also show the payment schedule. You may be able to arrange automatic premium withdrawals from your bank account. The withdrawal could be monthly, quarterly or semi annually. This allows you to spread your premium payment throughout the year as opposed to one annual payment. This arrangement may be without interest charges or a small one time service fee for the additional paper work involved.

The Insuring Agreement

This is a very brief paragraph which states that the insurance company will provide the coverage outlined in the policy upon payment of the premium, provided all the policy conditions and provisions are in compliance.

Definitions

It was mentioned earlier that the 'Easy Read' working uses 'you' and 'we' quite frequently. The definition section is designed to give the policy holder the meaning of some of the words used in the policy. Some words have the same meaning found in a dictionary, while others have a legal meaning which may be different than the common usage. This section clarifies any misunderstanding about the meaning of words or phrases used in the policy.

SECTION ONE – PROPERTY COVERAGE

Coverage A – Dwelling

This states that the property covered is the one described in the declaration, and that it includes any other structures attached to the dwelling. It also states that materials and supplies located within the property line are covered provided these materials are for repairs or to maintain the dwelling. Also considered a part of the dwelling are in-ground swimming pools, permanently attached equipment, an underground sprinkler system or a wall that is attached to the main structure, even if the wall is a part of a fence.

Coverage B – Other Structures

Other structures are sometimes called detached or appurtenant structures. These are non commercial building(s) within the property boundaries that are detached from the main house such as a garage, tool/utility shed or a changing room if there is a swimming pool. The coverage limit is 10% of the limit of Coverage A (main building). To illustrate, if the main building is insured for $100,000, the limit for all detached structures would be $10,000. Other examples will be explored in the Building chapter.

If the policy is a tenant's policy, there is no coverage for the building as the tenant is not the owner and has no financial interest in the building. You must have a financial interest in the object insured to have an insurable interest. To reiterate, financial interest means that if the structure is damaged or destroyed, a person or other entity would lose money. If the house is destroyed or damaged, the financial loss rests with the owner of the house, not the tenant. If a condominium unit is the subject of the policy, the reader will recall that it provides very limited building coverage, the costs of the betterments or improvements (upgrades) done by the owner and personal property (contents) within the unit. If the building is damaged or destroyed, the master policy covering the building structure and common areas would respond and pay for the repairs or replacement.

Coverage C – Personal Property

This section of the policy covers the personal property (contents) of the house, condominium or apartment. In the adjustment of contents losses, the procedure is the same if the contents are owned by the homeowner, tenant or condominium unit owner. Coverage is provided for your personal property while on your premises on an all risk or named perils basis depending on the type of policy purchased. It also covers your personal property away from your premises, but coverage is subject to a sub-limit. A policy providing $100,000 under coverage A (Building), may provide a payment limit for contents of 50% which would be $50,000 provided the policy was written on replacement costs (RC) basis. Some companies provide up to 70% of the building limit for contents coverage. Depending on the coverage purchased, you may be entitled to the actual cash value (ACV) of your contents. Contents coverage is subject to many sub-limits within the overall limit. To provide full coverage for certain items or types of losses regardless of the circumstances of the claim, could result in a moral hazard which means an insureds' careless or fraudulent nature.

It would be very difficult for an insurance company to reimburse an insured for large amounts of money allegedly stolen, or to be able to place a value on jewelry lost or stolen that was passed down through generations or similar types of losses. All companies limit losses for money, bank notes, gold, bullion, coins to $200. There are many other items listed in the policy that are subject to a sub-limit. If an insured wants to receive the full value for certain types of personal property, they can be 'scheduled,' meaning insured to value. Contents coverage also exclude motorized vehicles, boats over a certain size or weight, or boat motors over a certain horse power because these items should be insured separately by policies designed to provide specific coverage. In addition vehicles which are propelled by a motor can cause death or serious injury to persons or damage property of others. Since the homeowner/tenant/condo policies are not geared to provide broad liability coverage except for liability arising from the ownership or use of the premises, motorized vehicles and the like are excluded. Property of your tenants, roomers or boarders is not covered whether they live at your residence or reside at a residence owned by you at another location. If their property is damaged or lost, you have no financial or insurable interest. If however, the loss or damage is due to the condition of the premises, and you were aware of the condition due to personal observation or was told of the problem by the tenant, and you failed to rectify the condition, you may be found liable due to your failure to correct the defect. For example, you could be liable if a broken door lock was not repaired and as a result, the tenant's personal contents were stolen while they were away from the premises. Please see Chapter 6 for more details.

Coverage D – Loss of Use

In some policies this is called 'Additional Living Expenses.' If your home or the premises you rent is damaged by a covered peril, you may be forced to move out and live elsewhere while repairs are being done. This could be in a hotel/motel, a short term lease in an apartment or house, or staying with relatives or friends for a fixed payment. There are also other expenses which would not be incurred but for the damage to your residence. Increased costs for meals at a restaurant, use of a commercial laundry facility, temporary telephone or internet connection fees are covered. Since these are increased or additional expenses over and above what you would normally pay had there been no loss, they are called 'additional' living expenses. Your mortgage payments will usually continue while repairs are taking place, although a few lenders may suspend payments until you are able to return to your premises.

Another coverage included in this section is 'Fair Rental Value'. If you rent to others a portion of the house where you live, and because of a covered loss, both you and your tenant, (or just the tenant if only that section of the premises is affected) must move out in order for repairs to be done, your insurer owes the loss rent you would have collected less any expenses that do not continue. The payment for loss rent is in addition to what you would collect as outlined in the previous paragraph. You would collect your own additional living expenses if you lived at the damaged premises. The tenant cannot collect additional living expenses under your policy. If prior to the loss, the tenant moved out, you would still be entitled to loss of rent for the same rental amount paid by the previous tenant, provided you were trying to find a new tenant before the loss, and planned to do so after the repairs are completed. Payment stops when the repairs are completed, even if you do not have a potential tenant. Repairs must be completed within a reasonable time. The adjusting process under this coverage is explored in Chapter 7.

Additional Coverage

There are additional coverage that are available but may vary by company. The most common additional coverage are:

Debris Removal – If the cost to remove debris is not included in the dwelling (Coverage A) limit, this coverage allows up to an additional 5% of the limit of Coverage A to pay for debris removal.

Outdoor Trees, Shrubs and Plants – This is usually limited to 5% of Coverage A with a maximum of $250 per tree. Payment is limited to losses caused by perils named in the section and is not offered on an all risk basis. For example, damage by wind is excluded. To replace trees destroyed by a hurricane would be cost prohibitive.

Credit, Fund Transfer and Debit Cards, Forgery and Counterfeit Money – This section reimburses you for the unauthorized use of any of the cards issued to you or registered in your name. In case of a loss, you must comply with the reporting requirements of the bank that issued the card. If the reporting requirements are met, the bank will not seek reimbursement from you.

Forgery, alteration of a check or negotiable instrument – These types of losses are covered, as is acceptance in good faith of counterfeit money. This coverage is subject to a stated limit.

Inflation protection – During the policy term, the insurer will protect you from the effects of inflation as it relates to the cost of reconstruction of your home. Your insurer increases the amount of coverage annually to offset construction inflation due to the increased costs of materials and/or labour.

Fire Department Charges – Any charges by the fire department incurred in the fighting of a fire or other loss related activities. The maximum payable is usually $500.

Lock Replacement – In the event your keys are stolen, this coverage pays for the replacement or recoding of the locks in order to prevent future losses.

Readers are advised to check their policy as each policy type has different limits or additional coverage. Not all the coverage listed here are included in every policy, nor are the coverage limited to the amounts shown in this summary. If you are uncertain of your coverage limits, it is advisable to check with your broker or agent.

Perils Insured Against
If your policy provides 'All Risk' coverage, it means all losses are covered except those in the 'Exclusions' section, and is also subject to the policy 'Conditions.' A 'Named Peril' policy provides coverage in the event losses occur as a result of specific causes (perils) which are listed in the policy. There are usually between thirteen and twenty causes of loss listed. Although the perils are listed, there may be exclusions which may limit coverage or reduce payment. For example, the peril or freezing stipulates that heat must be maintained in an unoccupied or vacant dwelling during the heating season, or the water supply must be shut off and the system drained. By including that requirement in the policy, the insurer is limiting the exposure to a water loss claim. This prevents an

insured from turning off the furnace in order to save money before leaving the home to go on vacation, or not draining the system and subsequently making a claim for water escape caused by a pipe rupture due to freezing. Water leaking freely for days or weeks until the insured returns home could cause thousands of dollars of damage to the structure and contents. This requirement is also necessary if an insured has a summer cottage that is not occupied during the winter when heat should be maintained.

In the Canadian and U.S. policies there is no coverage for Water Escape, Freezing or Rupture if the dwelling is unoccupied for four (4) consecutive days unless you made arrangement for a competent person to check the house daily to ensure that heat is maintained (no furnace breakdown). The reasoning is the same as discussed above, and requires active loss prevention awareness by you. This requirement is waived however, if the water is shut off and the system drained.

If you have water damage caused by a leaking pipe in your home, coverage depends on the cause. If the pipe leaked because a weld broke, the cost to locate the leak (including repairing the holes made in the drywall) and the resulting damage is covered. If the leak was caused by rust or corrosion of the pipe, some companies will not pay for any repairs. Others will pay for the resulting damage only. The cost to repair/replace the pipe itself is not covered regardless of the cause as the item that caused the loss is not covered.

Exclusions
Property insurance is a contract of indemnity for sudden and accidental losses and is not meant to pay for repairs due to aging or wear and tear (maintenance). In addition, the policy is not meant to pay for upgrades or changes due to building code/ordinance requirements (see Chapter 9 for more on this issue). Also excluded are those types of claims which would be catastrophic such as war, nuclear accidents, earthquake, flooding and similar losses. No

insurer will provide coverage for war or nuclear accidents. Very few offer earthquake coverage which is subject to a payment limit and/or a high deductible. In the United States you can purchase flood insurance through the National Flood Insurance Program.

Some perils that are excluded may be removed from the list of exclusions. This can be done by purchasing an endorsement that overrides the exclusion. If a loss is not covered due to an exclusion, the adjuster should refer you to the relevant section of the policy during or after the course of the investigation.

Conditions

Conditions set the basis under which the contract will operate. You may recall that conditions are classified as General, Additional and Statutory. Some policies may have one category, most will have two or all three. Some states and provinces may require that statutory conditions must be included, while in other jurisdictions, statutory conditions are listed as general or additional conditions. The classification of conditions depends of the requirements of the Department of Insurance or the Department of Financial Services. Although it would be very unusual, if the state or provincial regulatory body does not mandate the category under which the condition must be listed, the decision is made by the insurance companies. Statutory Conditions are required by law as stated earlier in this book. If the state or provincial legislative body enacts laws requiring insurers to include certain conditions in their policies, an insurer would be in violation of the law if these conditions were not included in the policy as statutory conditions. The company would be subject to fines, or even the loss of their license to transact business in that jurisdiction. Lawmakers are sometimes forced to require that certain conditions are included by statute due to complaints from the public, as a result of case law or to ensure equal and consistent practices by insurers. Statutory conditions usually address issues of cancellation procedures, concealment or misrepresentation, material change, fraud, requirements after a loss, notice and proof of loss, salvage, entry and abandonment, appraisal, action against the insurer, when loss payable and notice or loss to the insurer. Each state or province also has the authority to add or remove procedures or requirements from that list.

The sections outlining the Conditions are straight forward and you should have little or no difficulty in understanding what is meant by each condition. The following is a quick interpretation of each of the conditions mentioned in the last paragraph with brief examples. These conditions may be classified differently in your own policy.

Misrepresentation – When an applicant for insurance provides false or misleading information on which the underwriter relies when deciding whether to accept or reject a risk. For example, when an applicant does not disclose their past claims history.

Concealment – When an applicant withholds material facts that would have changed an underwriter's decision regarding acceptance of the risk. Eg: when applying for a policy, not disclosing that the premises has extensive un-repaired hurricane damage.

Material Change – When there are changes in use of the insured property which makes the risk unacceptable to the insurer. Eg: after the policy is in force, an insured decided to start a home based business making fireworks. This would involve the storage of sulfur. Since this is a highly explosive substance, it creates an exposure that was not present at the time the application for insurance was accepted by the underwriter. If a fire ensues, even if it was not caused by the insurer's business activity, the loss would be far greater due to the storage of sulfur on the premises. That would represent a material change and would likely result in a denial of the claim by the insurer. The insurance company would correctly take the position that had they known of the insured's hazardous business venture, they would have cancelled the policy and would not have been exposed to a major claim.

Fraud – An insured who presents a fraudulent claim vitiates (destroys the value) of the entire claim. When an insured reports a burglary or theft of contents, an adjuster is assigned to investigate the claim. If it was discovered that only 5 of the 8 items reported stolen existed or were owned by the insured, the entire claim is voided. Even if the insured confesses and requests payment for the legitimate items that were stolen, there would be no payment. Although denying the entire claim may seem to be an unfair position, it is meant to discourage an insured from attempting to defraud the insurer, and if unsuccessful, still get the legitimate claim paid. Without that deterrent, the insured would have nothing to lose by his attempt to defraud his insurer.

Requirements After a Loss – The insured is required by this condition to promptly report any loss to the insurance company and to provide the necessary proof and supporting accounting or other documents to substantiate the claim. The insured must also state how and when the loss occurred and declare if there are other insurance policies which should also respond (to prevent double payment). If there is a second policy in effect, the payment is made on a pro-rata (proportional) basis by both insurers. If one of the two policies covering the same property has an excess coverage clause, this means that the policy would respond only after the other policy's limit (maximum payable) is exhausted. If the amount paid by the first policy is insufficient to pay the loss, then the second policy would make up the difference. If both policies had the excess coverage clause, the clauses would cancel each other and both policies would pay on a pro-rata basis to settle the loss.

Notice and Proof of Loss – Any written notice of a claim by the insured to the company can be hand delivered, sent by registered mail (recommended) to the agent or to the insurers' corporate or branch office. Notice must be given within a reasonable time after the loss. If you do not report a claim made against you by a third party to your insurer

34

within a reasonable time period, or if you wait until you are served with notice of a law suit, you may risk having coverage denied due to late notice. If you do not report the claim as quickly as possible, you are preventing your insurer from having the opportunity to investigate the claim promptly when the best evidence can be obtained or documented, which could be used as a valid defence. A Proof of Loss is a separate document and is not usually the initial report of a loss made by you to your insurance company. The Proof of Loss document is reviewed in more details in Chapter 9.

Salvage – The main requirement is that you must remove undamaged or salvageable contents from the loss site to protect it from further damage. The insurer must contribute on a pro-rata basis to the expense incurred by you to do so. After a full settlement of the claim, any item for which you were paid, ownership and possession passes to the insurance company who will dispose of the salvage and keep the proceeds of the sale. The only exception occurs if you are not fully indemnified. In that situation, your insurer sells the salvage and gives you a portion of the sale proceeds to fully satisfy your claim. An example of when this would occur is as follows. Assume you have a replacement costs limit of $50,000 under your personal property coverage. Following a loss, you were paid the full amount by your insurer, but the actual costs to replace all of the contents were $54,000. Your insurer took ownership of the salvage after you were paid, which was sold for $5,500. In order to fully satisfy your claim, your insurer should give you an additional $4,000 and keep $1,500. If your insurer was allowed to keep all the proceeds from the sale of the salvage, they would not have paid out the maximum $50,000 under the contents section. Their net payment would have been $44,500, ($50,000 less $5,500 credit from the salvage sale). Depending on the value of the salvage, the insurer may simply allow you to keep it.

Entry, Control and Abandonment – This Condition gives the insurer the right to enter the property to survey the damage, and to prepare an estimate or appraise the damage. It also stipulates that you cannot abandon the property (house or contents) to the insurer without the consent of the insurer.

Appraisal – In the U.S. policies, the appraisal procedure is outlined in the policy, while the Canadian policies stipulate that the insured has the right to request an appraisal in case of a dispute. Canadian insureds must refer to the Provincial Insurance Act where the procedure is outlined in detail. For Canadian readers, the procedures are as follows. If an insured disagrees with the values allowed by the insurance company with respect to the amount needed to repair or replace the damaged property, or the value of the property insured (including contents), either party can request an appraisal in writing after the insured files a Proof of Loss. The insured and the insurer will each choose an appraiser within 7 days after receiving the request for an appraisal (20 days in the U.S.). The two appraisers must appoint an umpire within 15 days (the same time frame in Canada and the United States). If they fail to agree on the umpire within the allotted time, a judge can appoint one. If the appraisers agree on an amount, their written reports are submitted to the parties in dispute and the claim is paid without the involvement of the umpire. However, if they fail to agree, the umpire makes the decision based on the reports of the appraisers. An agreement by any two resolves the amount in dispute. For example, if both appraisers agree on an amount, or if the umpire agrees with the amount of one appraiser, that becomes the settlement amount. In some jurisdictions, the decision from the appraisal process is binding, while in others, the dispute can still be litigated and decided by a court. In Canada, an insured can request an appraisal regardless of the amount in dispute, while in some states, the amount in disagreement is subject to a fixed minimum difference before an insured can proceed to the appraisal process. Disputed values of items that are stolen are not subject to the appraisal process as they are physically unavailable for appraisal. Each party pays their own appraiser and the cost of the umpire is shared equally by both parties.

Action Against the Insurer – This has the same meaning as 'Suit Against Us.' This states that no legal action can be taken against the insurer unless the policy provisions have been satisfied. It also stipulates that you have one year after the loss date to start legal action against your insurer. You should check your local jurisdiction as you may have a longer period in which to institute legal action, sometimes as long as 7 years.

Notice to Authorities – When a loss is caused by a criminal act such as theft, burglary, malicious acts or robbery, the insured is required to report the loss to the police. If an arrest is made, it gives the insurer the option to get a restitution order during the court proceedings against the guilty party.

Pair and Set – This means the insurer is only required to pay for the lost or damaged item if the loss involves a part of a pair or set. A lost ear-ring, or a loss of a piece from a set of cutlery would result in payment for one earring or to replace the lost knife or fork of the cutlery set. The insurer is not obliged to pay for the pair of earrings or the entire cutlery set.

Basis of Settlement – Unless the policy is written on a replacement cost basis, the insurer is liable for the actual cash value of the property/contents for which the claim is made. This is not to be confused with 'Actual Cash Value of Repairs.' Let's review an ACV of repair situation. When a building has fire damage, a repair estimate is prepared. Let's assume the repair estimate is $20,000. The insured decided not to repair the structure for whatever reason, and requests a cash settlement. He would be entitled to the actual cash value of repairs and not to the estimated amount. The amount that the insured is entitled to receive is computed as follows:

$$\frac{\text{Age of Building}}{\text{Use Life of Building}} \times \text{Loss} = \text{Payment}$$

If the building is 50 years old with a use life of 75 years, the payment is computed using the formula:

$$\frac{50}{75} \times \$20,000 = \$13,333.33$$

Subrogation – After payment of a claim, the insurer has the right to recover the amount paid from the party who caused the damage, unless the damage was caused unintentionally by the insured or anyone who meets the definition of an insured. This is called subrogation. The insured must cooperate in the recovery process. In some jurisdictions, the insured is paid a daily amount to attend the court proceedings if the insurer has to sue to recover from the liable party. In the lawsuit, the insured must be named as the plaintiff in the action. The insurance company cannot sue as the plaintiff because the direct loss was not sustained by the company, but rather by their insured. If the suit is successful, the money awarded by the court is given to the insurer as reimbursement for their payment to their insured. If the insured was allowed to keep the award, he would be compensated twice. The entire costs of the legal action are paid by the insurer.

Recovered Property – If any item is recovered after payment by the insurer, the insured or the insurer must notify each other of the recovery. This may occur following a theft if the stolen items are recovered, or if a scheduled item was later found by the insured after he reported the loss of the item. The recovered item becomes the property of the insurer. If the insured wishes to keep the recovered property, he must refund to the insurer the full amount paid to him unless the item was damaged which would allow the insured to deduct the cost of the repairs.

Mortgage Clause – This condition is explained in detail in Chapter 5. It is a separate policy issued to the mortgagee and coverage is unaffected if the insured commits a breach of the contract.

Appraisal – The appraisal procedure was previously explained in this chapter. Courts do not normally have the opportunity to appoint appraisers as the crux of quantum disputes are usually based on the difference of the repair/replacement figures by the appraisers already retained which triggers the appraisal process. Insured and insurers will usually use the appraisers who provided the original estimates in dispute.

As stated earlier, your policy may or may not have all of the conditions listed above. Inclusion of conditions depends on the requirements of your state or province, and the legislative laws that mandate conditions that are statutory.

SECTION TWO - LIABILITY COVERAGE
Coverage E – Personal Liability
If someone makes a claim against you alleging bodily injury or property damage, after an investigation to determine your liability (negligence), the insurer will pay up to the maximum shown on the declaration page under the 'Liability' section to settle the claim. The insurer is also responsible for the costs of defending you in court. However, once the insurer pays the maximum under this section, their duty to defend you or to make any further payment to the claimant ends. Chapter 8 provides more details.

Coverage F – Medical Payments to Others
The insurer agrees to pay reasonable and necessary medical expenses to others within three years of an accident due to bodily injury caused by the use or ownership of your premises. This coverage does not apply to the residents of the household except resident employees. In Canada, this section is called 'Voluntary Medical Payments' and is payable within one year (not three years) of the accident date. Payments are limited to $250, $500 or $1000, depending on the amount shown on the declaration page. This

allows the insurer to pay the necessary and reasonable medical expenses up to the limit, even if you were not negligent. This is sometimes referred to as a 'good neighbor clause.' Both U.S. and Canadian policies cover injuries caused by you due to unsafe conditions leading to an injury at your premises or caused by animals owned by you. There are extensive exclusions to sections E and F which are self explanatory.

Coverage G – Voluntary Payment for Damage to Property

This coverage is found only in Canadian policies. Like the voluntary medical payment section, this also allows payments to third parties for damage to their property even if you were not negligent. For example, if you were mowing your lawn and the mower's cutting blade propels a stone onto your neighbor's property and breaks a window. Each payment is limited to the least of the following:

The actual cash value of the damaged property

The cost to repair or replace the damaged property

The coverage limit (usually $200)

Your insurer cannot make a payment under any of the voluntary payment sections without your consent. If you do not consent to the payment, the party claiming injury or property damage must allege negligence and/or institute legal proceedings and prove that you were negligent. If this occurs, your insurer would investigate, and if satisfied that there was in fact negligence, proceed to negotiate and settle the claim without your consent. Your insurer would not need your consent as the payment would not be voluntary, but based on negligence.

The U.S. policies do provide coverage for 'Damage to Property of Others' under the Additional Coverage section. Maximum payment is $500, although some insurers do offer coverage up to $1,000. The payment can be made even in the absence of legal liability. It is a voluntary payment based on an insured's moral responsibility for causing the damage.

When you purchase a policy, you agree to allow your insurer to investigate, negotiate and pay claims made against you if you are legally liable.

Exclusions

The liability, medical, voluntary medical and property sections do have exclusions that are common to all sections. There are dozens of exclusions that are self explanatory. However, some of the important exclusions are as follows:

Criminal Acts – Bodily injury or property damage is not covered if it results from a criminal act by you or at your direction.

Intentional Acts – Bodily injury or property damage are also subject to exclusion from coverage if caused by intentional acts.

Punitive or exemplary damages are not covered. This means that if you are sued, and the court awards the plaintiff (person suing) monetary damages, and also an additional amount to punish you for your malicious, evil or fraudulent act, you are responsible for that portion of the award.

Allegations of sexual acts, physical punishment, mental abuse or the transmission of communicable diseases including Acquired Immune Deficiency Syndrome (AIDS) by anyone insured by the policy are excluded from coverage.

These are examples of four major exclusions. You should read the policy so that you are familiar with other exclusions, and if necessary, review them with your agent so that you will have a full understanding of the activities that are excluded from coverage.

SECTION TWO – ADDITIONAL COVERAGE

Under the Liability section of the policy, there is a limit to the amount the insurer will pay, which is the amount you requested when the policy was issued. The standard amount is $300,000.

You can increase the limit during the life of the policy for an additional premium. Usually, increases are requested on the renewal date of the policy. You are not allowed to increase the limit when a claim is pending against you. Over and above the limit, the insurer agrees to certain supplementary payments. For example, if the policy has a liability limit of $300,000, the insurer will pay up to that amount for an adverse judgment, plus expenses for the following:

Loss of Income while attending trial – Usually between $50 to $250 per day or as stated in your policy. It also pays for bonds or judgement premium, other expenses incurred by you at your insurer's request, and interest on the judgment. The Canadian policy reimburses 'reasonable expenses except loss of earnings.'

Costs for First Aid – Incurred for any injury covered by the policy except injuries sustained by persons insured under the policy. This is comparable to the 'Voluntary Medical Payments' section in the Canadian policies.

Damage to Property of Others – The maximum of $500, (or as stated in your policy) is payable when the damage is caused by you. This is similar to the section in the Canadian policies entitled 'Voluntary Payment for Damage to Property.' Intentional acts by you or at your direction will not trigger a voluntary payment, nor if the injury or damage is caused by your business pursuits, or from the ownership, use or maintenance of watercraft, or caused by motorized vehicles or aircraft. Golf carts are covered on golf courses while driving to and from cart storage areas and in private residential areas where there are golf courses.

You should review the other additional coverage in your policy.

SECTIONS ONE and TWO - CONDITIONS

There are 9 or 10 Conditions that apply to both sections of the policy. Depending on the state or province in which you reside, some of these conditions may appear as statutory or additional conditions. A summary of these conditions are outlined below.

Policy Period – This states that coverage for property damage or bodily injury is effective only during the policy period.

Fraud or Concealment – There is no coverage if you withhold relevant information or make false statements or engage in fraudulent activities.

Cancellation – This tells you what you need to do to cancel your policy. The cancellation procedure by the company is also explained. There are time sequences when coverage is still in effect before the cancellation takes effect. This period of continued coverage gives you time to obtain insurance elsewhere.

Non-Renewal – This is often confused with the cancellation of a policy. Cancellation takes place during the policy period. Non renewal takes place at the end of the policy period and the company elects not to renew the policy for a new term. The company must provide written notice to you of its intention not to renew 90 days prior to the date the policy expires. This notice also gives you time to seek coverage with another company. The insurer only has to provide proof that the notice of cancellation or non renewal was mailed to you to prove that you were notified.

Assignment – This condition prohibits assignment without the written consent of the insurer. Assignment means transfer of interest from one party to another. For example, if you had a fire loss and owed money to a friend, you cannot instruct your insurer to pay the proceeds of your claim to your friend to satisfy your debt. Insurance is a personal contract, and the insurer is not obligated to negotiate with or pay any other party except those named in the contract or a person who successfully filed a claim against you. Similarly, if you sell your home, you cannot assign your homeowners insurance to the purchaser.

Liberalization Clause – If an insurance company revises the policy in order to broaden coverage without additional premium, the broader coverage will immediately apply to all similar policies in effect at that time.

Waiver or Change of Policy Provisions – Any waivers or changes are not valid unless it is in writing from the insurer. You cannot make any changes to the policy provisions.

Death – If a named insured dies, the policy will continue to insure the legal representative of the deceased insured. This coverage however is restricted to the premises and contents of the deceased insured.

Subrogation – An insured may waive subrogation rights in writing against a person or entity. This must be done prior to a loss. Such waivers are necessary when government bodies are involved.

SECTION TWO – CONDITIONS

There are Additional Conditions that are applicable to Section Two only:

Limit of Liability – This states that the maximum payable for any one occurrence (an event) will not exceed the limit shown on the declaration page. This applies regardless of the number of persons injured. To illustrate, you have liability limits of $300,000 and while you were entertaining guests, you had an open bar allowing your guests to serve themselves. As a result, an impaired guest driving home was involved in a collision due to his impairment, and seriously injured multiple occupants in another vehicle. They successfully filed a lawsuit against your guest and you, alleging you were negligent under the host liquor liability tort. Regardless of the severity of the injuries, the maximum that can be paid by your insurer is $300,000. If your insurer does not want the responsibility of determining how much each claimant should receive, the $300,000 can be paid into court. The court would review the medical reports and decide how much each plaintiff should receive. As reviewed earlier, if the judgement against you is in excess of $300,000, you are personally responsible to pay the additional amount of the award. Your insurer would pay the court costs and legal fees to defend you.

Duties after a Loss – Basically, these are the same as the requirements under Section One. It specifies that you will:

Give prompt written notice to the insurer or agent outlining the circumstances of the loss, including the place, time, person(s) involved, witnesses and their addresses.

Forward immediately every complaint, summons, statement of claim or any other legal notice or document you receive.

Fully cooperate with your insurer in their investigation of the claim, and if required, attend all hearings, discovery, deposition and trial.

Not make payment(s) to the claimant or admit to, or assume any liability.

Submit a sworn Proof of Loss if you are suing your insurer, and make available the damaged property in your possession or located elsewhere, for inspection by your insurer.

Suit Against Us – This is a repeat of a previously mentioned condition stating there can be no legal action against the insurer unless the policy provisions are met. It also specifies the time frame in which legal action must be commenced.

Duties of an Injured Person – Coverage F
The injured persons or their representative must authorize the release of medical records, provide proof of claim under oath if required, and submit to a medical examination of the insurer's choice as requested (known as an independent medical examination – IME).

Payment of Claim – Coverage F
Payment to an injured person under this section is not an admission of liability.

Bankruptcy of an insured will not terminate the obligation of the insurer under the policy.

Personal Liability – Coverage E – Other Insurance
This coverage is excess over any other insurance. This means that if you have any other insurance policy that would respond to the loss, the maximum payable under that policy must be exhausted before this policy would respond.

Severability of Insurance – If the policy covers two insureds, and there was a suit against one, the policy would protect and defend the insured that was sued as if each had separate policies. This does not however, increase the limit (maximum) payable if there is an adverse judgement.

Some policies use the word 'Provisions' instead of 'Conditions,' both of which are interchangeable. They both mean stipulations. It is in your best interest not to violate the Conditions/Provisions of the policy.

Over and above the coverage offered by the Homeowner, Tenant or Condominium Unit Owners' policies, you may have a special need for altered coverage. You can remove certain coverage from your policy or for an additional premium, special coverage if

available, can be added. These changes are called 'Endorsements' or 'Riders.' A few examples of endorsements that would PROVIDE coverage if not included in the policy are:
1. Ordinance/Building Code Upgrade increased costs.
2. Replacement costs on building and contents.

Endorsements that would REMOVE coverage are:
1. Injury caused by trampoline use.
2. Flood or earthquake exclusion.
3. Existing damage exclusion.
4. Animal liability.

Insurers may not always offer endorsements to include or increase coverage. For example, the amount payable for stolen money, gold, bullion and the like is limited to the maximum amount as stated in the policy. If you want to increase that limit, there is no endorsement available to do so. Insurers do not provide increased limit for these types of losses as they do not want to expose the company to large losses involving money or precious metals. It would create a 'moral hazard' (the temptation for an insured to present a fraudulent or exaggerated claim). Other types of endorsements that are readily available are detailed below.

Schedule – This is an endorsement that increases the amount payable or provides additional coverage for certain items in your home. For example, jewelry, a stamp collection, cutlery, furs etc., which are subject to various sub-limits may not compensate you for the full value if there is a loss. In addition, if the item is lost or damaged, (a ring that can't be found, or a camera that falls overboard on a fishing trip), are the types of losses that would be payable as the Schedule gives all risk coverage. By scheduling each item, you are not only paid more than the sub-limit imposed by the policy, you are also given coverage for losses that would normally be excluded. Scheduling of contents is also referred to as 'Personal Articles Floater.' This is explored in more detail in Chapter 6.

Fine Arts Coverage – This is specifically for art, sculptures and other similar pieces of value. This endorsement has the same effect as the Personal Articles coverage. These articles are usually written on a 'Valued' basis which means that in the event of a loss, the insured is paid the predetermined amount shown on the endorsement.

In both the Personal Articles and Fine Arts coverage there are exclusions. Wear and tear, deterioration, defects, property illegally acquired, kept, transported or subject to seizure for breach of any law, musical instruments used for a fee, intentional or criminal acts by the insured or at his direction, electrical damage except when caused by lightning, war and nuclear incidents are the usual exclusions that apply to this coverage.

Mass Evacuation – Additional Living Expenses
This coverage provides reimbursement if there is no damage to your home, rented premises or condo unit, but you are required by the authorities to evacuate your neighborhood due to an accident that endangers the area. For example, a train derailment and/or explosion while carrying dangerous chemicals resulting in the release or threat of release of noxious fumes in the environment which may cause respiratory problems, serious illness or death. This coverage is available in Canada but not in the United States due to the population density.

Earthquake Coverage – There is no coverage for damage caused by earthquakes. It is also very difficult to get this coverage by endorsement. If companies do not want that type of exposure, they are not going to offer it by endorsement. In very few states or provinces is this coverage available. Although earthquakes do not pose a serious risk in most areas, it is listed as a standard exclusion. If you are able to obtain coverage by endorsement, it states that in addition to the primary earthquake, after shocks that are within 72 hours will be considered a single event. There are separate deductibles for each section of the policy (building, detached private structures, and contents), and the coverage does not include damage by flood or tidal wave caused or aggravated by an earthquake. Usually, there is only one deductible if there is a single cause of loss, but earthquake coverage has multiple deductibles although a few companies may offer the coverage with one large deductible. Fires caused by severed gas lines, downed electrical power lines or any other sources of ignition caused directly by the earthquake are covered. In the endorsement, this is referred to as 'fire following,' which means a fire caused by and following an earthquake.

Water Damage Extension – If this coverage is included or purchased by endorsement, it covers damage caused by the backing up or escape of water from a sewer, sump, septic tank, eaves trough (gutters), downspout or the melting of ice or snow on the exterior of the roof. It does not cover loss caused by water seepage or leakage of water below the surface of the ground including through sidewalks, driveways, foundations, walls, basement or other floors, windows and other openings, or while the dwelling is vacant or under construction even if your insurer issued a 'vacancy' or 'course of construction permit.' Damage caused by water that runs or pools on the surface of the ground or from streams, rivers, lakes, creeks, pools, ponds or any other bodies of water is not covered.

Boat, Motor and Trailer Coverage – This provides coverage for the above items and miscellaneous accessories within the continental United States and Canada. It provides Named Peril coverage, but can provide coverage on an All Risk basis for an additional premium, subject to certain exclusions. It can also be purchased to provide Replacement Costs or Actual Cash Value coverage. You should check your policy and/or discuss these options with your agent.

SINGLE LIMIT POLICIES

You will note that on your policy Declaration page, the various limits for each coverage are shown. It shows coverage limits for

Building, Other Structures, Personal Property, Loss of Use, Personal Liability and Medical Payments. Throughout the policy, the various sub-limits for each coverage category are also shown.

Some insurers offer a Single Limit policy. It allows full payment for a loss even if the limit of a specific coverage is exhausted. For example, assume the following:

	Limit	Loss	Payment
Building	-$100,000	$75,000	$75,000
Other Structures	- 10,000	12,500	10,000
Personal Property	-50,000	56,000	50,000
Total		$143,500	$135,000

You would have an uninsured loss of $8,500 because the Other Structures and Personal Property coverage are insufficient to cover the damage or replacement costs. The single limit policy would apply the remaining amount left on your building coverage (since you would still have $25,000) to pay for the other structures and personal property shortfall.

CHAPTER 5
Section A Building

The next four chapters detail the adjustment procedures and policy interpretation of the Building, Other Structures, Personal Property (Contents), Loss of Use and the Liability sections of the policy. By examples, you will get an understanding how the policy is interpreted during the adjustment of a claim, and the reasons for certain procedures that an adjuster must follow. There are literally hundreds of case law involving the policy sections and wording. These decisions handed down by the courts over the years, in addition to the state or provincial insurance laws, form the framework for the interpretation and procedures used by adjusters. Since each state and provincial courts sometimes interpret the policy wording differently, it would only confuse the reader to quote those cases. There are however, some cases that are recognized to be precedent setting, that is, earlier court decisions used as a guide by judges in deciding subsequent cases with similar facts. Some of the principles established in those cases are used in the examples given, although the cases themselves are not cited, which means the names of the parties involved, the state or province, or the year and legal reference (case numbers) are not specifically mentioned. The reader must also remember that new case law is ongoing, and some of the decisions referenced in this book may have since been overturned. Since the court decisions were not handed down by the United States or Canadian supreme courts, the decisions may not be binding in your state or province. The reasons for certain actions by insurers or adjusters are also explained.

This chapter deals with the Building section of the policy. As mentioned previously, coverage can be purchased on an 'All Risk' or 'Named Peril' basis subject to the policy exclusions. The policy is written to respond to direct loss or damage. A fire, hurricane or other such perils that cause partial damage or results in a total loss of a building are considered direct losses. If you discover that your house was unknowingly built on a site which is contaminated, and because of environmental laws which came in effect after you purchased the house, you may be prevented from selling the house, or the resale value has decreased. There is no coverage as the house is not damaged and would not be a direct loss.

If you have replacement cost coverage, the cost of the repair is paid in full subject to the policy deductible. For example, under normal weathering conditions, an asphalt shingle roof should last between 15 to 30 years depending on the quality of the shingles purchased, or the climate in your area. Shingles deteriorate faster if subject to severe changes in temperature. Let's assume you purchased '20 year use life' shingles. If the roof sustains hail damage, the insurer must determine if it should be repaired or replaced. If the decision is to replace the roof, and the roof is ten years old, it means that the insurer should pay one half of the replacement cost as you have already gotten ten years of use. Since insurance is supposed to place you in the same position you were before the loss, paying a half of the replacement costs would make sense. Replacement cost however, requires your insurer to replace the roof without applying a depreciation factor and consequently, the insurer must pay the entire cost of replacement less your deductible. If the cost of replacement is $5,000, without the replacement cost option, the insurer would pay $2,400 ($2,500 less $100 policy deductible), and you would pay $2,600. Under the replacement costs option, you would pay the $100 policy deductible, and the insurer would pay the remaining $4,900. In some areas, the policies provide coverage for roof covering and siding on a depreciated basis (actual cash value), as insurers may not offer the replacement cost option in that area. This may be due to frequent hail storms which would require the insurer to pay full replacement costs repeatedly over a relatively short period of time. In that situation, you would receive $2,400.

To obtain the benefit of the replacement cost coverage, there are requirements that must be met. At the time of the loss, the amount of insurance carried on the building must be at least 80% of the cost to rebuild the entire structure. To compute whether this requirement was met, the adjuster reviews the application submitted by the agent. The application has a section showing the calculations done by the agent before it was submitted to the insurer. There is a standard formula with regional modifiers used to arrive at a replacement cost figure for the area in which the house is located. Once the adjuster is satisfied that the amount of insurance equals 80% of the replacement value, no penalties are applied. The repairs are paid in full without deduction for depreciation. If the house was under insured, you would pay a penalty. Lets work through an under insured situation. Assume a replacement cost of $200,000. You should have coverage of $160,000 (80%), but had only $140,000. If you sustained a loss of $70,000, the payment by your insurer would be calculated as follows:

$$\frac{\text{Did Have (\$140,000)}}{\text{Should Have (\$160,000)}} \times \text{Loss (\$70,000)} = \text{Payment (\$61,250)}$$

You would have a penalty of $8,750 as your insurer would not pay the full $70,000. This is called co-insurance. If you do not insure to the correct value, you will pay a share of the loss which is a co-insurance penalty.

Another reason for a co-insurance penalty is based on fairness. Assume there are two houses of equal value but insured No. 1 insures for one half the value, while insured No. 2 insures for the correct value. They both sustain losses of equal amounts. It would be unfair to reimburse them equally since insured No. 2 paid a higher premium based on the correct value, while insured No. 1 paid less premium based on an incorrect value. Consequently, insured No. 1 pays a penalty when he has a loss.

Note that the 80% calculation does not include the value of the land, excavations or supports, pipes, drains or wiring that are underground. You also have the option of waiving the replacement costs provision and settle on an 'Actual Cash Value' basis. The settlement amount under an actual cash value is computed in the following manner. The amount for the repairs is depreciated in relation to the age of the house. An example of the calculation was shown in Chapter 4.

Subsequently, if you decided to repair the structure, you have a year from the date of loss to present your claim for the full replacement costs to your insurer. You must complete the repairs and either present documentary proof that repairs have been done, or allow an inspection by the insurer's representative. The insurer will then pay the least of:

1. The building coverage limit of the policy
2. The amount spent to effect repairs
3. The replacement costs for the damaged part of the structure using materials of like kind and quality.

On the market today are policies that offer 'Guaranteed Replacement Costs.' This means that if a house sustains major damage, the insurer will pay over and above the stated policy limit to repair or replace the structure. The main factors that could result in a higher repair costs are unexpected price increase for materials, labour rates or transportation of the materials if the house is located in a remote area. There is an additional premium charged for this coverage, and there are three conditions that must be met:

1. There must be no reduction of the initial coverage amount at the time the policy was first issued or subsequently renewed.
2. You must notify the company within 30 days if any additions are made to the structure which increases the value by 5% or more, unless the amount spent is $5,000 or less.
3. You have complied with the two (2) conditions stated above.

The guaranteed replacement cost coverage increases the building limit and does not increase any other coverage limits.

o paint the walls
). The repair costs
making the total
) above the policy
ng to save money,
policy limit which
position is that the
ctorily to washing
:umstances would
may elect to get a
t fixtures or make
ld bring the repair
obligated to write
the proper repair
situation is having
is of the walls and
pooing would be

l' is another issue
ends coverage if a
or no more than 30
premises will be
ly for a 'Vacancy
mited time. This is
e obvious reason is
into or vandalized.
he house are away
house is devoid of
ie courts have ruled
n life, it cannot be
th minimal contents

age Clause. When a
end money for the
t there is continuing
asset. In addition, a

when the debris results
ed loss, the removal of
debris results from the
ir property, or if you are
ction debris, there is no
aused by a peril such as
ie amount allowed for
If the building coverage
t for debris removal of
debris removal amount
e than $300,000. In that
,000, you would be left
ture.

ling coverage relates to
ey are covered up to a
'ayment is limited to a
and is capped at $250
iove the tree. There are
in the policy. You will
hurricane, tornado and
to remove and replace
following a windstorm
iere is limited coverage
ing, and is still resting
The cost incurred to
se which is damaged in
:ompany however, will
n authorized landfill or
by a listed peril.

a significant role when
mple, a building has an
e, the adjuster writes a
igure is accepted by a
ie adjuster has allowed
) for shampooing the
s and shampooing the

carpets, neither can be cleaned satisfactorily
and replace the carpets costs an additional $6,
which were $45,850 have increased by $6,0
repair costs $51,850. This new amount is $1,
limit. The insured takes the position that by t
the adjuster has caused the repairs to exceed t
the insured must pay on his own. The adjuster
walls and carpeting may have responded sati
and shampooing. A solution under those c
require some type of compromise. The insure
carpet of lesser quality, or less expensive li
some other cost reduction decision which w
amount within the policy limit. The adjuster
the estimate based on his best judgement c
technique. One method of avoiding this type
the cleaner or contractor test clean small sect
carpet to determine if cleaning and sha
successful.

Determination of 'Vacant' versus 'Unoccup
that could create a problem. The policy sus
house is vacant. Some policies allow vacancy
consecutive days. If you anticipate that yo
vacant for more than 30 days, you can ap
Permit' which your insurer may issue for a
usually approved on a one time only basis. T
that an empty house is more likely to be brok
'Unoccupied' means that the inhabitants of
temporarily, while 'Vacant' means that the
people or furnishings. There are cases where
that if a house has enough contents to susta
considered vacant. This means that a house w
could be considered unoccupied and not vacar

In the Building section of the policy is a Mort
bank, loan company or private individual
purchase of a house, there is a requirement th
valid insurance on the property to protect the

Mortgagee Clause is also required as it treats the mortgagee as a separate insured. If an insured has a loss and decided not to repair the structure, the mortgagee can file a proof of loss and demand that repairs are done. Similarly, if the insured violates any of the policy conditions or provisions that may void coverage, the mortgagee's rights are still protected and either repairs must be done, or the mortgagee must be paid the full amount of the repairs in order to maintain the value of the collateral. For example, if an insured commits arson (deliberate burning of the structure) and is charged criminally, he may or may not be convicted. The mortgagee is not barred from payment although arson is a violation of the policy condition unless it can be proven that the arson was committed by the mortgagee or at the direction of the mortgagee. There may be no criminal arson charges laid against an insured due to insufficient evidence, but the insurer may still deny coverage based on suspicion of arson. In the criminal court, guilt must be proven beyond a reasonable doubt while in a civil action, one only has to prove the probability of guilt. If the insured sues the insurance company for payment and is successful, the claim must be paid. If the insured loses the case, the denial stands. Regardless of the result, the mortgagee is paid. If the insurer successfully defends the suit, the company has the right to recover the amount paid to the mortgagee from the insured by initiating a law suit if necessary. In extreme cases, the insurer can pay the balance of the outstanding loan to the mortgagee and assume ownership of the property. The insured has the option of reimbursing the insurance company to regain ownership, or the insurer can sell the property to recover the payment made to the mortgagee.

Another issue faced by insureds and insurers occurs when there is deliberate damage done to the premises (arson/vandalism) by one of the parties who jointly owns the property. If a policy is issued to Mr. and Mrs. Joe Public, and Mr. Public deliberately sets the house on fire (arson), there is no coverage because it was an intentional act. But the situation gets more complex when it is alleged that Mr. Public acted on his own, and consequently Mrs. Public was an innocent party and should be paid. The courts have ruled both ways on this issue. In some cases, the court has taken the position that the actions of one insured affects the status of the other uninvolved party, and both are barred from recovery since the policy was issued in both names. Other court decisions stated that as joint owners, both have an equal financial interest in the property, and since one party was not involved in the arson or vandalism, that party is entitled to a 50% payment of the amount of the damages.

In other cases similar to the above scenario, the situation is further complicated by the alleged state of mind of the person who intentionally damaged the property. Some courts have allowed full payment based on expert testimony indicating that the individual who committed the offence was insane, temporarily insane, intoxicated or under the influence of a mind altering substance (drugs), and consequently was not able to form a criminal intent as he would be unaware of the consequences of his actions.

Other building claims that are bothersome involve color matching of roof shingles, colored sidings and carpeting. Quite often, an adjuster will take the position that the only amount owed is to replace the damaged shingles or sidings, or that carpeting of the same color that is laid throughout a house does not justify complete replacement if only one area is damaged. The adjuster may also point out that the policy responds to 'direct damage' and consequently the insurer's obligation is to replace the damaged portion only. This can create friction during the adjustment of the claim, particularly when both parties hold firm positions on the issue. These conflicts can be resolved by compromise. If the new shingles create a quilt like appearance due to the fading of the original shingles, there are options available to the adjuster. He could allow complete replacement of the slope that is most visible from the street, usually the front of the house, or pay the roofer to remove shingles from the rear of the roof (already faded), and install them on the visible front slope, and use the new shingles on the rear of the roof where the color difference is less visible. The insured should bear in mind that the color of the new shingles will also fade over time and the color difference will become less obvious due to the weathering process. The same rationale applies to vinyl/aluminum siding. Some manufacturers are making these products color fast (non fading).

If there is a carpet color matching dispute, it can be resolved by using a doorway as the logical cut off point between the old and new carpets. Adjusters are trained to use common sense in the adjustment of claims. They are constantly reminded that if a repair technique would be unacceptable had it been their own home, it would also be unacceptable to an insured, and other solutions should be explored. It would be highly unusual for an adjuster to force an insured to accept a repair when the color difference is extreme and very obvious. Some companies may offer an 'appearance allowance.' This is a monetary offer of an amount over and above the repair/replacement costs, to induce the insured to accept the slight color difference in the carpeting, siding or roof shingles. If the impasse cannot be resolved at the adjuster level, perhaps a branch or head office claims supervisor with higher decision making authority should be involved.

Another troublesome area in the adjustment of building or contents claims involves scorching. Quite often, a hot pot placed on a kitchen counter made of formica or other plastic type material will result in a circular or semi-circular brown mark on the counter top. Clothes in a dryer that are discoloured by over heating due to a defective timer, or clothes being ironed when the temperature is set incorrectly for that particular type of fabric, may all result in a claim due to scorching. The adjuster will reject these claims as there was no fire, and will invoke the 'Application of Heat' exclusion. Fire is defined as combustion producing heat and light. Since scorching is technically not a fire, the denial is valid.

However, there are circumstances when scorching is a legitimate fire claim. For example, if a kitchen counter top shows signs of charring anywhere in the scorched area, particularly at the edges, there is a strong presumption of light and heat (light being a flame which generates heat), and consideration should be given to the claim as a fire loss. In addition, the insured should be asked if a flame was observed, however briefly.

The new synthetic materials used in some types of carpets will not ignite. Instead, they will melt and form a hardened mass. If an insured has a claim involving a burn on a synthetic carpet, (eg: a log falling from a fireplace onto a carpeted floor), the adjuster may take the position that the damage was caused by scorching, since there would be no sign of a traditional burn pattern. Most companies will accept the hardened mass as evidence of a fire and pay the claim.

There are two classes of fires. There are friendly fires and hostile fires. Friendly fires are those that are intentionally ignited for normal domestic use and remain within controllable confines. Examples are cooking fires in or on a stove, or fires in a fireplace for heat. Hostile fires extend beyond their control area causing damage to property and are legitimate insurance claims. By agreement, insurers recognize cigarette burns as fire claims without placing the onus on the insured to prove heat and light, even if the discarded cigarette only caused scorching.

'Loss Assessment' must be claimed during the policy period. If a Condominium Corporation, an Association of Property Owners or a Home Owners Association, impose a loss assessment against association members to repair damages caused by a covered peril, your policy will pay the assessment up to $1,000 or the maximum amount stated in the policy. Assessment that is imposed by any governmental body is not covered.

CHAPTER 6

Section B Personal Property

This chapter explores the adjustment of personal property claims (contents) and some of the difficulties caused when proof of ownership is an issue. It was previously mentioned that the contract of insurance is based on 'utmost good faith.' It is worth repeating that both parties to the contract are expected to be honest and open in their dealings with each other, particularly when a claim is presented. At the onset of the contract, the insurer does not send an inspector to examine and verify the contents of your house prior to accepting the risk. It is assumed that you are being truthful, and based on that good faith you are accepted as an insured.

Also previously reviewed were the different types of policies and whether they provided all risk or named peril coverage. You may also recall that all risk means that payments would be made for all types of losses except those subject to exclusions. Named perils means that the loss or damage must have been caused by a peril that is specifically listed in the policy.

There are sub-limits for payments if some of your personal contents are lost or damaged. If the maximum payable for the total loss of all the contents in your house is $60,000, without sub-limits on certain items, you could claim the full $60,000 for the loss of one single valuable item such as a rare stamp, a very valuable coin, an expensive piece of jewelry etc. With the exception of money, bank notes, bullion, gold and the like, you can 'schedule' items that are subject to sub-limits, which not only would allow payment for the full value of the item, but also provide all risk coverage subject to exclusions that are listed on the schedule.

In most cases, it also guarantees the amount you would receive if the article was lost or destroyed. On some schedules, if an item is valued at $5,000, it will have a 'V' written next to the item. It means that there is an agreed value confirmed by an appraisal, and the amount shown would be paid by the insurer in case of a loss. This is called a 'Valued Schedule.' Not all schedules are valued. The most common schedule states that the insurer will reimburse the insured for replacement of the item up to the maximum amount shown on the schedule, or the replacement cost, whichever is less.

For example, if a ring is appraised by a qualified jeweler or gemologist and valued at $5,000, the amount shown on the schedule would be $5,000, and the appropriate premium is charged. If the ring is lost, the insured would expect $5,000 to replace it. The adjuster may send the appraisal kept in the underwriting file to a jeweler the insurance company uses to replace or make custom jewelry that is lost. Due to the volume of business sent to these jewellers, along with the high mark-up, they can usually give the insurer discounts for replacements. In this example, the jeweler may inform the insurer that the ring can be replaced for $3,250, applicable tax included. The insurer instructs the insured to go to the jeweler in question to have a duplicate made for $3,250. The insured demands $5,000, and takes the position that it was the appraised value and scheduled amount. The insurer points out the schedule's provision which states that the insurer is liable to the maximum of $5,000 or the replacement costs, whichever is less. Because the jeweler can replace the ring for $3,250, that is the amount owed by the insurer. If there was a 'valued' schedule in effect, the insurer would pay $5,000 without determining the cost of the actual replacement. When the replacement ring is selected or custom made, the insured can take it to a gemologist, along with the original appraisal of the lost ring to ensure that the replacement ring is of the same quality and value.

The adjustment may get even more complex. Assume the insured agrees to accept $3,250 instead of replacing the ring. Some insurers may offer a lesser amount by taking the position that the replacement value quoted by the jeweler included state, provincial and/or federal taxes which is not incurred unless the replacement purchase is made, consequently the tax is owed to the government and not to the insured. Most companies however, will simply pay the replacement cost including tax, even if the insured does not replace the item as the tax was paid by the insured when the original purchase was made. Jewelry has a relatively high mark up, and it is possible to replace an appraised piece of jewelry for much less than the original price and maintain the same quality and value through a discount or wholesale source.

In certain situations you may recover the full value for your jewelry above the sub-limit even if they were not scheduled. If you own jewelry valued at $8,000 and elect not to have them appraised and scheduled, your policy's sub-limit for jewelry loss is $2,000. If the jewelry is stolen, the maximum you could collect is $2,000, but if you had a major fire loss and some or all of your jewelry were destroyed and/or inadvertently discarded when the debris was removed, you would still be able to collect the full value of $8,000 provided you have proof of ownership, and your total contents claim would not exceed the coverage limit. The sub-limit is applicable only if you have a jewelry theft claim.

It is also possible for you to recover more than the scheduled amount following a loss. Let's assume you scheduled a piece of jewelry for the appraised value of $6,000. Over the years, because it has become an antique, the value appreciated to $7,500. It is subsequently stolen and the insurer pays the scheduled amount of $6,000. Since theft is one of the insured perils under the policy with a sub-limit of $2,000, you can collect the additional $1,500 under the theft coverage since in this situation, both the theft coverage and schedule would respond to the loss. This would not occur if the loss was classified as mysterious disappearance which is excluded in most policies. The schedule covers mysterious disappearance and would trigger payment of the appraised value of $6,000, but unlike theft, which is covered by the policy, there would be no additional amount paid since mysterious disappearance is an excluded peril. If the policy covered mysterious disappearance, then as in a theft loss situation, the insured would recover the full value of $7,500.

Insureds sometimes confuse a 'schedule' and a 'personal articles floater' which are not the same. A Personal Articles Floater, sometimes called a Personal Effects Floater, is a separate policy that is usually purchased by individuals who travel frequently and want a separate policy to cover their personal effects on a world wide basis. As an example, a member of a band who wants to cover his musical instrument and other property while on tour. This limited policy does not provide coverage for your items while at your residence.

An item brought into the country by a returning resident who did not declare the item at customs in order to avoid import duties and/or taxes, can create adjustment difficulties if the item is subsequently lost or damaged due to a covered peril. The item would have been subject to seizure if at a later date, customs became aware that no duty or taxes were paid at the time it was brought into the country. The insurer can deny the claim if during the investigation it was discovered that the item was smuggled into the country. The policy states that there is no coverage for property illegally acquired, kept, stored or transported, seized or confiscated for breach of any law. Since customs would have seized the undeclared item had they known it was being smuggled into the country, the insured has transported and kept the item illegally, and consequently there is no coverage. However, once the period for seizure by customs expires (three years in some jurisdictions), the goods are no longer illegally kept by the insured, and the insurer must pay the loss as the exclusion would no longer apply. An insured cannot offer to pay the customs duty after the loss in an effort to place the item in legal status retroactively. This issue affects anyone who does cross border shopping. However, since the implementation of the North American Free Trade Agreement (NAFTA), a lot of custom's restrictions have been lifted and duties removed. A call to your state or provincial customs office or on their official web site should clarify all issues regarding importation and duties.

A claim made under the credit/debit card, fund transfer card, forgery and counterfeit money coverage, is usually as a result of theft and may also cause some confusion. The insuring agreement states that the insurer will pay up to $500 for the 'legal obligation' of an insured to pay, (meaning to repay the bank or credit union), because of theft or unauthorized use of credit or debit cards issued to an insured, or loss resulting from theft or unauthorized use of a fund transfer card used to deposit, withdraw or to transfer funds. There is no deductible applied to this coverage. The key words are 'legal obligation.' Let's examine two situations to determine the legal obligation issue. Insured A has a bank account with a balance of $2,000. His card is stolen, and $800 is withdrawn from his account. He submits a claim under his policy. The sub-limit under theft of money is $200 and the maximum payable under the credit/fund transfer coverage is $500. The insurer accepts the loss as $800. Insured B has an account balance of $50. Because he has arranged overdraft protection of $1,000, the felon is also able to withdraw $800. Like insured A, he too makes a claim under his policy. Insured A loses $600 while insured B is liable to the bank for $750. The insurer reimbursed insured B because of his legal obligation to the bank. Insured A had enough funds to cover he stolen $800 in his account, and is not liable to the bank for the stolen money, so his claim was limited to the maximum payable for theft of money which is $200. Insured B only had $50, and consequently he was legally liable to the bank for $750. As a result, his insurer paid the maximum allowed of $500. He is still liable to the bank for the remaining $250 as he had $50 in his account. He can't be legally liable to himself for his own stolen $50. The adjuster computes the loss as follows:

Insured A		Insured B
$2,000	Bank Balance	$50
None	Overdraft Protection	1,000
2,000	Cash Available	1,050
800	Stolen	800
200	Paid under money theft coverage	50
0	Paid under 'legal liability'	500
200	Total paid	550
600	Personal loss	250

This coverage requires that you must comply with the bank's terms and conditions regarding notice of theft or misuse of any bank card immediately upon discovery of a fraudulent transaction, or under certain circumstances, within the stated period of time outlined in the card agreement. Prompt notice to the bank will negate any responsibility on your part. It is very important that you read your bank's 'Terms and Conditions' to familiarize yourself with the requirements regarding illegal use of the card(s) and any penalty that may apply.

One of the policy Conditions in the section entitled 'Our Option' gives the insurance company the right to repair or replace any part of the damaged property with materials of like kind and quality. A written notice from your insurer is sent to you within 30 days after they receive your Proof of Loss. Although rare, this may occur if you and your insurer disagree on the scope of repairs (what needs to be done), and/or the quality of the materials. Rather than go through the appraisal process to resolve the impasse, your insurer may invoke their option. The danger to the insurer is that they are assuming all responsibility for the repairs, and they are liable for any additional costs if you are dissatisfied with the quality of the material used or workmanship. Your insurer must pay to correct any problems even if the costs exceed the policy limit.

Some policies cover 'Mysterious Disappearance' although most do not. Scheduling an item would provide coverage for mysterious disappearance. Mysterious disappearance is defined as the disappearance of an object from a known place within a known time frame under unexplainable circumstances. For example, Mrs. Insured makes a claim for a missing bracelet. She last wore it to a wedding two weeks prior to its loss, and she recalls putting it on the shelf in the bathroom on her return from the wedding. She doesn't know exactly when it went missing, but she could not find it when she wanted to wear it again. She has had no visitors, nor have there been any work men or strangers in the house within the past two weeks. That is a classic case of mysterious disappearance. It is a judgement call by the adjuster after he has completed his investigation. If there is a strong presumption of theft, he may elect to pay the claim as a theft loss. He would have considered other factors before making his decision. Were there other equally valuable pieces of jewelry in the same area that were not taken? Was their cash in the vicinity which was untouched? Who had access to the house? The answer to these and similar questions would assist the adjuster in determining if it was a mysterious disappearance or theft. If the policy provides coverage for mysterious disappearance and the facts support the presumption of a mysterious loss, after obtaining statements from the insured and others to determine the loss circumstances, the loss would be quantified and paid.

After a personal property claim is paid, who is entitled to the salvage? If your home was burglarized, vandalized or items were damaged, stolen and recovered, the understanding is that once you are paid for your loss, the damaged items or the items subsequently recovered belong to the insurer as salvage. The insurer sells the damaged or recovered items and keeps the proceeds. This is not always the case. If you had jewelry stolen that were valued at $15,000 and the items were not scheduled, your insurer would pay $2,000 which is normally the sub-limit for jewelry losses (although some companies do have higher sub-limits). A few weeks later, an arrest was made and some of the stolen jewelry valued at $5,000 was recovered, who owns that salvage? In this example, you would. An insurer is not entitled to the salvage until you are fully compensated. In other words, after the insurer paid you the maximum $2,000, you would still have an uninsured loss of $13,000. The recovered jewelry would belong to you to offset your loss. If the jewelry was scheduled, and the insurer paid the full value or replaced all of the stolen pieces, the recovered pieces would belong to the insurer because the insured would have been fully compensated. See Chapter 4 (page 35) for additional information on salvage.

The main area of disagreement and dispute between an insured and insurer may be proof of ownership. Your insurer has a right to require proof of ownership, and an insured must be able to provide such proof. Following a major fire, an insured may claim that all the contents in the house are a total loss and demand payment up to the limit of the policy under the personal property (contents) section. The adjuster, during his on site investigation, takes photos and/or a video of the damaged contents, lists the contents of each room taking care to note brand names and model numbers if they are legible for future valuation. Sometimes, this is not always possible as a major fire can destroy contents so severely that it is impossible to list some of the items by going through the debris. An insured may be provided with 'Contents Schedule' forms and asked to make a list of all the contents from memory. Some adjusters take a video of the debris that may assist in identifying items if there are disputes later in the adjustment process. Some companies require that the adjuster sit with the insured during the preparation of the contents schedule forms in order to avoid the insured providing a list with exaggerated values. Remembering all the contents can be difficult, particularly since the insured may be in a state of shock following the event and distraught over the loss of items of sentimental value that cannot be replaced. Quite often, the list is not completed for weeks as the insured and family members try to remember every item that was in the house. This can also occur when an insured suffers a theft loss. Some items may not be missed until the insured wants to use or wear them, and at that time, they are discovered missing long after the theft had occurred. The adjuster will try to get as much information from the insured as possible in an attempt to determine the value of the destroyed or stolen articles. He may require the brand names, model numbers, date of purchase, place of purchase, method of payment and the amount paid for the item. What he is trying to establish are; (a) the quality of the item and (b) whether the item was in the premises or was owned by the insured. Unfortunately, not all insureds are honest. Some will make a claim for items they never owned, or exaggerate the quality or price. Most insureds are honest, but some do not regard cheating on insurance claims as a crime. It is insurance fraud. They rationalize their actions as simply trying to recover some of the premiums paid over claim free years, and when there is a claim, taking the opportunity to do so. At times, these are the same individuals who complain the loudest when premiums are increased, and see no relationship between their dishonest actions and the need for increased premiums. It is the insuring public that eventually pays for dishonesty or exaggerated claims in the form of higher premiums.

Listed on the next page are examples of the documentation an insured can provide to prove ownership:

1. Receipt from the establishment where the item was purchased
2. Credit or debit card receipts
3. Cancelled check(s)
4. Warranty cards
5. Ownership manuals *
6. Bank statement showing the date and appropriate withdrawal on or about the date the item was originally purchased
7. Original packaging of the item – boxes
8. Photographs, DVDs or videotape of the items

> * Ownership manuals instruct the purchaser how to operate the product as opposed to a brochure or pamphlet which only advertises the product's features. If a purchaser loses the manual, some companies have their products' manuals on line which can be downloaded. If the manual is a downloaded copy, the adjuster may require additional proof of ownership.

All banks must retain financial statements for seven years to comply with the Income Tax Act in the event of a tax audit and you are required to produce financial statements. Most people do not keep records for seven years, but banks can provide copies of bank statements or checks to prove purchases and prices of items in dispute.

If necessary, the adjuster will obtain statements from friends or neighbors who may be able to confirm having seen the disputed items when they visited the insured. This is usually done as a last resort, and may be done with or without the permission of the insured. It is not necessary for the adjuster to get permission from an insured to carry out any investigation he deems necessary.

The adjuster may look through the insured's photo album, videos or DVDs taken at family gatherings, which may show expensive candle holders, cutlery or other claimed items in the background.

In some instances the insured may have already taken a video or photos of each room in the house, or used one of the many firms offering their services to document the contents of the home for insurance purposes.

Adjusters in the course of their investigation look for evidence or clues to confirm ownership. He may take measurements of the wall unit or entertainment center shelving to determine if the television/stereo/vcr/dvd or other pieces of electronic equipment could fit in the space where the insured claimed the items were kept. The same applies to the number of records/tapes/cds/dvds allegedly stored on shelving in a wall or media storage unit. He examines the carpet to determine if the item for which a claim is made rested in that area of the room and left an indentation.

If the reader thinks that filing a claim will automatically subject you to a criminal type of investigation, you are incorrect. The majority of dwelling/personal property claims are settled routinely. It is only when the insured's version of the alleged facts are vague or inaccurate, that a more in depth investigation is undertaken by the insurer. For example, an insured that allegedly made recent expensive purchases and have no documentation, or is claiming the loss of high priced electronic, computer, stereo or camera equipment, but cannot recall the prices, places and dates of purchase, model names or even the operational features. Companies that specialize in underwriting high valued homes with expensive contents adjust claims differently. Shortly after the policy is written, they have qualified staff appraisers who visit the insured's home and document the contents before a loss. The photographs, video tapes, dvds and appraisals are kept in the underwriting file for future reference. The values are updated periodically and used if necessary in the adjustment of any claims.

Some adjusters will incorporate a 'life style' observation while at the insured's home. For example, an insured who reports the theft of very expensive items in contrast to the contents of the home, who lives in a less desirable area and has a low or no income, may result in the adjuster doing an in depth investigation. If there is sufficient proof of ownership, the claim would be routinely processed and paid.

Let's review the difference between Actual Cash Value (ACV) and Replacement Cost (RC) of contents and the adjustment calculations. This was briefly addressed in the replacement costs paragraph in the Building chapter. It is worth repeating that if you have ACV coverage, you are entitled to the actual cash value of the property, which is the current replacement cost, less depreciation. To illustrate, if a chair purchased 5 years ago for $500 is the subject of a claim, the insurer owes the current price of a similar new chair, less past usage. The insurer would establish the 'use life' of the chair (10 years in this example), the current replacement cost ($800) and using those figures, determine the ACV. Payment is calculated as follows:

$$\frac{\text{Age (5 years)}}{\text{Use Life (10 years)}} \times \text{Replacement Price (\$800)} = \text{Payment (\$400)}$$

You will note that the original cost was used only to determine the current cost of a chair of like kind and quality. If the replacement price had remained at $500, the payment would have been $250. If you have replacement cost coverage, you must replace the item in order to qualify for the full replacement cost. If you decided not to replace the chair, you are only entitled to the ACV of $400. If you buy another chair at a later date, you can submit the invoice to your insurer and receive the additional $400. All payments are subject to the policy deductible.

Most policies allow one year for replacement of items, while others allow 180 days. You can apply for an extension of time giving the reason for the request, and the insurer has the option of extending the time allowed, but that time frame would not be unlimited. It is best to make the request in writing which would remove any confusion when the purchase is eventually made and a supplementary claim submitted. A few insurers are offering replacement costs coverage without the necessity of replacing the item.

Following a loss, is it possible to get an upgraded item and receive the full payment from your insurer? The answer is yes. New electronic equipment like stereo systems, computers, cameras, cell phones, flat screen televisions and similar items have upgraded or additional features within a short period of time after the original model is replaced on the market by the manufacturers. As a result, it may not be possible to replace the exact model of the lost or damaged item, and an upgraded model with enhanced features would have to be purchased, even if at a greater cost to satisfy the claim. In most cases, as these newer models gain popularity, the prices are reduced, and in some instances are sold at a lower price than the original model they replaced.

If you purchase furniture on credit and there is a loss, your insurer is not obligated to include the lien holder on the settlement check. That obligation only exists in the case of a mortgagee, not a lien holder.

Some furniture companies will self finance the furniture sold on credit. To ensure payment if the item is damaged or stolen, they will also include an insurance policy to protect the value of the item, and the premium is added to the selling price. This is underwritten by a licensed insurance company. If there is a loss, the insured must declare if there is more than one policy in effect. The claim payment is not shared equally by both companies, but rather on a pro rata basis. See example below:

Policy A – Homeowners – Personal Contents $100,000
Policy B – Furniture   15,000
Loss of Furniture   10,000
Total insurance available $115,000

72

Policy A pays: $\dfrac{\$100{,}000}{\$115{,}000} \times \$10{,}000 = \$8{,}695.65$

Policy B pays: $\dfrac{\$15{,}000}{\$115{,}000} \times \$10{,}000 = \$1{,}304.35$

Each company sets the standard of proof of ownership it will accept. It depends on the company's philosophy, and how rigid they are regarding proof. What might be acceptable to one company may be inadequate for another. Because of this, some insureds may complain that they are being treated unfairly when it's really an issue of the company's approach. If you are unhappy with the manner in which your claim was handled, there are options available and these are reviewed in Chapter 9. You may consider changing your insurance company to avoid problems in the adjustment of any future claim.

You may also recall that when negotiations fail, there is the appraisal procedure that was reviewed in the 'Building' section of this book. When dealing with personal property disputes, the procedure is the same. It also involves the use to two appraisers and an umpire. The cost sharing is the same, with each party, (you and your insurer) paying your own appraiser, and sharing equally the cost of the umpire.

CHAPTER 7
Section C Additional Living Expenses or Loss of Use

This section will examine in detail the 'Additional Living Expenses' and 'Loss of Use' coverage. This coverage reimburses you for costs you would normally not incur if you did not have a loss. There is dual coverage within this section. The first reimburses you for the additional expenses to maintain your normal standard of living elsewhere while repairs to your home are being done. The other coverage provides fair rental value for that portion of the house that was rented or held for rent, and is uninhabitable due to damage caused by a covered peril (fire, vandalism etc). Fair rental value payment ceases when repairs are completed, and not when the tenant moves back in the house or a new tenant is found. Repairs must be done in a timely manner, and delays caused by you will not lengthen the period of coverage. Deducted from the payments are expenses that do not continue. For example, if there are separate meters for water and/or electricity and you do not incur these expenses while the tenant is living elsewhere, those amounts are deducted by the insurer. These expenses are called 'non-continuing.' If the tenant cancels the lease following a loss, there is no coverage beyond the period it would take to repair the premises and have it available for tenancy.

If you are claiming Additional Living Expenses, you are expected to maintain your normal spending habits. Some expenses are not reimbursable, such as long distance telephone calls, entertaining others, alcohol charges and the like. At the beginning of the adjustment of the claim, the adjuster will take a statement from you listing your normal expenses. When the repairs are completed, and you return to your dwelling, at that stage you would submit your additional living expense claim. A comparison is made of your normal living expenses prior to the loss to determine if you maintained your usual spending habits. You should keep all receipts in a large envelope, (some insurers provide one), to ensure that they are not misplaced. If you want to present your claim in an organized fashion, you should separate the receipts by date or type;

hotel, meals, laundry, gasoline etc. Your expenses can be submitted to your insurer on a prearranged schedule, particularly if the repairs to your residence will take a long period of time. This would give you funds on a weekly, bi-weekly or monthly basis. Payment is calculated by determining your normal pre-loss expenses and paying the difference. These are your 'additional living expenses'. The most common additional expenses involved in loss of use claims are:

- Additional transportation costs if you are temporarily living farther away from your place of business, or the increased amount for fuel costs to commute to work and/or to take your children to school
- Hotel, house or apartment rental costs
- Additional costs for laundry using commercial facilities
- Surcharge by the hotel for local telephone calls
- Meal expenses provided by restaurants
- Additional heating/electrical cost due to exposure to the elements while repairs are being done to your home.

Depending on your situation, there could be additional expenses not mentioned above.

If you rent a furnished house or efficiency apartment which has a stove and a refrigerator, you would not be eligible for additional meal allowance as you could purchase groceries and prepare meals as you normally would at your own home. Undamaged pots, plates, utensils and other necessities from your home could be used while at your temporary location. If these items were damaged beyond use at your home, new ones should be purchased under your contents coverage (you would be replacing these items eventually), and this would allow you to provide home cooked meals. If you incur charges for temporary hook up for telephone, natural gas, cable/satellite television and electricity at the temporary residence, those expenses would be reimbursable. If your household consists of a large family, it would be more economical to relocate to a short term rental apartment or house instead of renting multiple hotel rooms. There are rental agencies that specialize in short term leases. Your insurer may also have a list of agencies they have used successfully in the past. If you anticipate any expenses that may be considered unusual, in order to avoid problems later in the adjustment process, you should discuss them with your adjuster as soon as possible after the loss to avoid unexpected surprises. This may involve an ongoing medical situation of a family member that requires special arrangements, or you may need to send your family pet(s) to a boarding facility while your home is being repaired as some temporary locations do not allow pets and some may add a surcharge.

If your policy term expires while repairs to your house are still on going and you decide not to renew with the same insurer, the insurer on risk at the time of the loss must continue to pay your additional living expenses until you return to your home.

Some companies provide coverage for up to two weeks for additional expenses if your local civil authority prohibits access to your premises due to damage to neighboring premises by a peril insured under your policy, even if your house is not damaged. For example, your policy provides fire damage coverage for your home. If your neighbor's house is damaged by fire, and you are not allowed to remain in your home, you would be entitled to additional living expenses. This may occur if your home shares a common wall typically found in a semi-detached house, town homes, apartments or villas.

Some policies also provide 'Mass Evacuation Additional Living Expenses.' Evacuation orders must be issued by an official body, such as the Federal Emergency Management Authority (FEMA), or any civil official authorized to do so. You are covered for up to two weeks from the date of the order and a maximum payment of $1,000. If the order was issued due to an earthquake, flood, tidal waves, tides or the overflow of any body of water (natural or man made), or the war/nuclear incident exclusion, there is no coverage as these causes of loss are not covered in your policy. This coverage only applies if the order is a result of a peril covered in your own policy even if your home is undamaged. Only a few companies offer this coverage in the United States due to the population density in some states. For example, mandatory evacuation when a hurricane is approaching a very populated area would be very costly.

Every insured is obligated to mitigate their loss. This means every attempt must be made to make the loss less severe financially and/or protecting the damaged or undamaged property from additional damage.

CHAPTER 8

Section D Liability

This chapter deals with the liability coverage provided by the policy. You will recall that the policy provides protection for the insured for legal liability, and also for voluntary payments for bodily injury or property damage as outlined in Chapter 4.

You are liable for bodily injury or property damage when you have acted negligently, and as a result of such action, someone suffers an injury or damage to their property. Negligence is defined as a failure to exercise that degree of care which the law requires to protect others from an unreasonable risk of harm. If someone acts negligently, they can be found legally liable for injury to others or damage to the property of others. In a lawsuit, the injured party or the owner of the damaged property is called the 'claimant' or 'plaintiff,' while the person causing the injury or damage is referred to as the 'defendant.' The plaintiff has the onus to prove negligence by the defendant.

There must be a direct connection between the negligent act and the property damage or injury. In some jurisdictions, if the injured party also acted negligently, the court will reduce the monetary award by the percentage of negligence of the injured person. This means that if the injured party acted carelessly and was partially responsible for his own injuries, a court may find him 30% negligent and reduce the monetary award to 70%. This is known as 'comparative' negligence. There is a rarely used statute called 'contributory' negligence. This means that if there is any negligence, however small by the plaintiff, he would recover nothing for his injury. 'Gross' negligence means that by a person's extreme reckless actions, he had no regard for the safety of others.

Examples of negligence by individuals are illustrated in the following situations:
A visitor to the insured's home falls and injures himself when he trips over toys left on the stairs by the insured's young son. A

visitor is injured when he slips and falls on an icy driveway that was not shovelled, salted or sanded by the homeowner long after the snowfall ended, and he had ample time to do so. If however, the homeowner had a contract or arrangement with an individual or company to clear the snow from the walkway or driveway within a certain time after the snowfall and failed to do so, they may be found liable because they failed to perform the snow clearing service as dictated by their contract with the homeowner. If an infant drowns in an insured's swimming pool, depending on the circumstances and relationship with the infant, the insured could be held liable. If a swimming pool is not in a fenced area and can be seen by an infant who is not on the insured's property, its accessibility could create a situation called an 'attractive nuisance'. This means that the pool is an attraction to infants and creates a danger to their safety. Attractive nuisance could also be a large discarded appliance left on your property or at the curb to be picked up by the sanitation department with the door still attached, resulting in an infant locking himself in it and suffocating. In most jurisdictions, an infant is anyone under the age of eighteen years. Host liquor liability exposure, referred to in the Application chapter in this book, can also be considered negligence. All of the above are examples of potential negligence by an insured which may result in legal liability. That does not mean that the defendant could not have a valid defence against the allegation of negligence which his attorney would argue at trial. In cases where the defendant is in violation of local laws, it is even more difficult to avoid an adverse judgment. For example, some communities have laws that state that all swimming pools must be fenced, or that doors on discarded appliances must be removed.

If the plaintiff alleges negligence in the complaint or statement of claim, the insurer must provide a defence against the allegation, even if the allegation has no basis, and must pay the entire costs to defend the insured. If there is no allegation of negligence, the insurer has no obligation to defend their insured. For example, following an assault, a plaintiff alleges in the pleadings (a legal document filed in a lawsuit) that the assault was an intentional or criminal act by the insured.

The liability section is subject to a limit the insurer will pay in the event you are found negligent. The limit is usually $300,000, but this amount can be decreased or increased by paying a higher premium. If you are sued for an amount in excess of the policy limit, your insurer must advise you in writing that any court award (judgment) in excess of the policy limit is your responsibility. If a court awards an injured party $350,000, and the policy limit is $300.000, you are personally liable for the remaining $50,000 to satisfy the award. For the small additional cost to increase the liability limits, the reader is well advised to do so. A large judgment in excess of the policy limits can result in financial ruin. Another reason why you must be advised that the complaint or statement of claim seeks monetary damages that exceeds the policy limit, is to give you the opportunity to retain your own attorney if that is your decision, to protect your financial interest over and above the policy limit. Most often an insured will consent to having the attorney retained by the insurer to represent both. The letter sent to the insured is called an 'Excess' letter. It means exactly what it's called. It advises the insured that the plaintiff is claiming an amount in excess of the coverage limit.

The exclusions under the liability section were reviewed in Chapter 4. The reader should be aware that the homeowner/tenant/condo unit policies will pay the legal costs to defend you if you are sued for negligence. Those costs are over and above the policy limit.

Tenants can be legally liable for negligence if the loss circumstances are the same as the examples cited for homeowners. They can also be liable to their landlords for damages to the rental property, even if it were not done intentionally. If a tenant is cooking and forgets to turn off the stove while on the telephone, and as a result there was a fire which damages the rented premises, the tenant would be negligent and liable to the landlord for the costs of the repairs. The tenant would also be liable for any damages to other neighboring residence if the fire spread to their home or apartment. If the landlord's insurer paid to repair the damages, the company would pursue the tenant for the amount paid for the repairs. This is called subrogation. Depending on the circumstances of the loss, a tenant may also be liable for damages caused by their guests.

Activities by infants may result in liability claims against them and may include the parents. If the infant is very young, the court would decide if the infant knew the difference between right and wrong by questioning the infant at the start of the trial or hearing, and/or rely on experts for their opinion after they interviewed and evaluated the level of the infant's intelligence. In some jurisdictions, infants cannot be sued if they are below a certain age which may vary by state or province. On the other hand, even if the infant is very young, the court may rule that the parents were negligent by not adequately supervising the activities of the infant, and that lack of supervision makes them liable. In that situation, the policy would pay the damages to the plaintiff as the parents were found to be legally liable. Depending on the facts of the case, the court could order restitution (payment) by the parents for the damage. This type of payment for damages would not be reimbursable by the insurer as it is meant to make the parents personally accountable for their lax supervision.

CHAPTER 9
Adjusting Issues

This chapter contains some guidelines and other information to assist you in understanding how and why the adjuster makes repair and coverage decisions. It also provides options when there is a disagreement with the adjuster and suggests ways to resolve the impasse.

Hailstorms can occur anywhere in the United States or Canada, but the central areas of the continent are more susceptible. Depending on the size, hail stones can cause damage to composition shingles. The damage is caused when hail stones puncture the membrane of the shingles, resulting in leaks causing interior damage. The size of the hail stones, the intensity of the storm (if wind driven), and the age of the shingles, are all factors affecting the severity of the damage. If the shingles are relatively new, they could withstand the storm with minimal damage. Composition 3 Tab shingles are rated for 15, 20, 25 or even 30 years. You may notice a 'sand like' substance in the eave trough (gutter) after a hail storm. Those are actually the granules dislodged from the surface of the shingles by the hail stones. These granules give the shingles their strength. It may appear that there is no damage to the roof, however the roof life has been shortened. You should negotiate an allowance with the adjuster for the loss of 'use life' of the shingles. For example, suppose you replaced your roof 5 years ago with new 20 year shingles. The use life of the shingles may have been shortened by 5 years due to damage by the hail storm. Instead of having to replace the roof in 15 years, you may have to replace it in 10 years. It is the loss of 5 years of use life that allows you to negotiate a monetary allowance with the adjuster. Regardless of the type of roof on a building, it can be damaged by hailstones. Built-Up 3, 4 or 5 ply, galvanized, metal, roll roofing, tile or wood shakes are all susceptible to hail damage and should be inspected after a hail storm, even if it appears there is no damage when viewed from the ground.

If a window or door is left open, and rain causes interior damage to the building (warped wooden floors, damaged drywall etc.) and/or to your personal contents, there is no coverage. Coverage only applies if the wind caused the 'opening' allowing wind driven rain to get into the premises. If the wind blew down a tree or propelled an object which damaged the door or window causing an opening that allowed rain to get in, the damages would be covered. The same would apply if your roof covering was blown off or damaged causing interior water damage. Some companies may deny the claim if the shingles lifted (hinge like effect) due to the force of the wind, allowing the wind driven rain to get under the shingles and the water leaked between the seams of the roof sheathing into the interior of the house. Because the shingles were undamaged and laid flat on the sheathing once the wind subsided, that is the basis for the denial. The rationale is that the wind did not cause the 'opening'. Some companies however, would pay to repair the damage and not use the 'cause of the opening' as a reason for a denial of coverage.

Your personal contents are covered anywhere in the world. Some policies provide contents coverage away from your premises but only if the property is 'temporarily removed.' The reason for the temporary removal wording was to provide coverage for student's personal contents while attending university away from home. It allowed students to take their personal contents that were covered while they lived at home with their parents, and still have coverage at another location while attending university. These items were considered temporarily removed as it is assumed that after graduation, the students would return home with their contents. If there was a loss while the student was living away from home, and the student did not plan to return home to live with his parents, there would be no coverage since the property would not be 'temporarily removed.' There is a downside to that concept. Suppose you purchased a watch while on vacation in France. The watch was stolen when someone broke into your hotel room. A report was made to the police in France, and on your return home, you filed a claim with your insurer. Your claim would be denied as there would be no coverage because the watch must have been at your permanent residence, and temporarily removed (on the trip), with the intent to return with the watch to your residence. Since it was purchased when you were in France, it was never at your residence, and consequently was not temporarily removed. The new policy wording corrects that problem by providing world wide coverage by using the phrase 'temporarily elsewhere.' By changing 'removed' to 'elsewhere,' the policy covers the student even if there is no intent to return home after university, and also covers items purchased abroad.

Coverage for items away from your residence is limited to 10% of your contents limit or $1,000, which ever is less. Some enhanced policies have a limit of 10% or $2,500, which ever is less.

It is accepted that the insurer is not liable for the cost to upgrade a building to meet current building code requirements enacted into law after the structure was built, unless you purchased the code upgrade endorsement. These codes may involve electrical wiring, plumbing or construction upgrades to make the structure stronger to withstand natural disasters like a hurricane, earthquake or similar events. When you have a loss, the state or provincial building inspector will not issue a repair permit unless the new code requirements are included in the repair estimate. In some jurisdictions, the courts have held that if an insurer sells a policy with *replacement cost coverage*, the code upgrades are a part of the repair process, and not withstanding the code upgrade exclusion in the policy, the insurer must pay the additional cost for the upgrades as the building inspector will not allow the repairs to be done unless it includes bringing the building up to code. This means that the insurer must pay the full amount, even if the insured does not have the code upgrade endorsement. This would not apply if the insured purchased a policy providing *actual cash value coverage*.

Suppose at the time of the original construction, a house did not conform to some of the building codes in force at that time. Subsequently, the home owner buys a policy and purchases the code upgrade endorsement. The structure is damaged by a peril (fire), and in order to obtain a repair permit, the building must be brought up to the current code. Some insurers have taken the position that the costs of the code upgrades are the responsibility of the insured because when the building was originally constructed, it was in violation of the code. In other words, the insurer is only liable for code upgrade changes that came in effect after the building was constructed, and not the code violations at the time of the original construction.

In the United States there is an organization funded by the insurance industry called the National Insurance Crime Bureau (NICB). In Canada, the organization was known as the Insurance Crime Prevention Bureau (ICPB), which is now a part of the Insurance Bureau of Canada. The responsibilities of these organizations are to assist insurers that do not have an in-house special investigations unit to investigate insurance fraud, to keep records of claims and to provide claims history and statistical data to underwriters. These staff members are primarily former police officers, firemen or fire investigators who can assist adjusters or fire marshals in the investigation of suspected fraudulent or arson claims. It is one of the resources used by insurers in their fight against fraud. The information in their data base is provided by member companies (insurers), using a standard reporting format. Some insurance companies have an in-house Special Investigative Unit (SIU) staffed with similar types of investigators, or they may also have staff adjusters specially trained to investigate fraud.

A 'Proof of Loss' form is the document providing basic information through which an insured presents a claim to his insurer. When dealing with small claims (an upper limit of approximately $5,000), insurers will normally waive the necessity of filing a proof of loss, but they are mandatory in large or suspicious losses. The proof of loss is a first party document. Only an insured, or in some cases a mortgagee may file a proof of loss. A third party, (someone claiming against the insured) cannot file a proof of loss as there is no contract between a third party and the insurer. When an insurer pays damages to a third party on behalf of a negligent insured, the insurer obtains a release. A release is a document signed by a third party stating that the third party has

85

accepted a monetary amount in full settlement of a claim, and releases the insured and insurer from any further claim. A release closes a claim by a third party, while a proof of loss is a notice to an insurer by an insured that opens a claim under the insurance contract.

The Insurance Act/Law differs by state and province. Normally, once an insurer receives notice of a claim, a blank proof of loss must be provided to the insured within 60 days or earlier if requested by the insured. When the proof of loss is completed and returned to the insurer, the insurer will either reject the proof of loss (in writing), or pay the claim within 20 days after receipt of the document if there is an agreement regarding the amount claimed. If the proof of loss is not rejected by the insurer within 60 days after it is received, there is a misconception that the amount claimed is deemed to be accepted by the insurer, and the full amount claimed must be paid. This is incorrect. After 60 days, if the claim is not paid, the insured can initiate a law suit. The insurance Law or Act in each state or province stipulates the time an insured has to file suit. The time frame varies from one year to as much as seven years after the loss, depending on the type of claim and the jurisdiction.

If the proof of loss is rejected, the insurer must state in writing the reason for the rejection. If it was rejected because the insurer quantified the loss at less than the amount claimed, the insurer will keep the proof of loss and send a letter to the insured stating that the proof is accepted, but the amount claimed is rejected. If the proof is rejected because sections of the form were incorrectly completed, the letter from the insurer should outline the defects on the proof, return a copy of the defective proof and a new form so that the insured can resubmit a properly completed form. In that situation, the 60 day period in which the insurer has to accept the claim starts when the new proof of loss is received by the insurer, not the date when the defective or rejected one was received. If the proof of loss is accepted, the claim is paid in the normal fashion. If it is rejected, and further negotiations fail, the insured or insurer can serve written notice of their intent to proceed to appraisal (discussed earlier), arbitration or file a law suit. Acceptance of the proof of loss by the insurer does not mean that coverage may not be an issue or that the insurer agrees that the policy was in force at the time of the loss. In some instances, the insurer may require a sworn or notarized proof of loss. This may be due to a large pending claim payment to the insured, subrogation potential by the insurer against the liable party or a suspected fraudulent claim.

Another document used by the insurer is a 'Non Waiver Agreement.' If you have a loss, and the preliminary investigation indicates that the loss may not be covered, you will be asked to sign a non waiver agreement. This form states that the insurer has the right to investigate the loss, but reserves the right to deny coverage if the investigation leads to the conclusion that the loss is not covered by the insurance contract. By getting your signature, the insurer is protected if you later claim that because the adjuster conducted an investigation into the loss, you were led to believe that the loss was covered, and the insurer has estopped itself from denying coverage. The issue of estoppel was examined in Chapter 3.

If you refuse to sign the non waiver agreement, the insurer can send a 'Reservation of Rights' letter to you which has the same effect as a non waiver agreement. The reservation of rights letter states that the insurer reserves the right to investigate the loss and may deny coverage at the conclusion of the investigation without creating an estoppel. Basically, it is a unilateral version of the non waiver agreement.

Mobile homes must not be confused with motor homes. Motor homes have an engine and are considered motor vehicles licensed to be driven on public roads. They are covered by an automobile insurance policy which is not the subject of this book. Mobile homes are pre constructed residential premises situated on land owned or leased by an insured. They can be moved by being placed on wheels and/or transported by a flatbed truck to a new location. Most mobile home policies are written on an actual cash value basis, although a few companies do offer full replacement cost coverage. Built in furniture and other attached household items are considered a part of the mobile home. Some policies have limited hailstorm coverage which requires that hail stones must puncture the exterior membrane (roof and/or siding) for coverage to apply. Dents caused by hail stones are not covered. The method used to settle a total loss involves locating a used home similar to the one destroyed. If the policy provides replacement cost coverage, the insured is given enough funds to purchase a new one with similar features. Some policies exclude awnings, outdoor antennas and equipment, whether or not they are attached to the mobile home. Some policies on the market will cover these items on an actual cash value basis. If there is a mortgage, the policy also includes a mortgage clause which protects the mortgagee.

CHAPTER 10
Hurricane Issues and Tips

A hurricane is defined as a windstorm of sufficient violence capable of damaging property either by the force of its own winds, or by projecting objects against it. For hurricane coverage to apply, the storm system must be declared a hurricane by the National Hurricane Center. A hurricane occurrence begins at the time of a hurricane watch or warning and ends 72 hours following the termination of the watch or warning issued by the National Hurricane Center.

You can reduce your hurricane premium which is shown separately on your insurance company's invoice if you select a high deductible or if your home has:

- Removable roof turbines which can be capped
- Reinforced garage door(s)
- Hurricane shutters or impact resistant windows and doors
- Hurricane straps which helps to hold the roof structure to the exterior walls
- Diagonal 2"x 4" bracing between the gable end and the roof trusses
- Roof covering (shingles or roof tiles etc.) in good condition

The unique feature of hurricane coverage is that it has a deductible that is separate from the policy deductible for other perils. Hurricane deductibles are between 2% and up to 10% of the building limit. If the coverage on your building is $300,000, a 2% deductible would be $6,000, and at 10%, it would be $30,000. This means that if your dwelling is damaged by a hurricane, you would be responsible for the first $6,000 or up to $30,000 of the repair costs, depending on the deductible percentage you chose. It is very difficult to find a company offering the standard $500 deductible that would include hurricanes. Policies sold in states that are likely to experience more than one hurricane per season have a Calendar

89

Year Hurricane Deductible endorsement. This endorsement explains how the hurricane deductible is applied if there is more than one hurricane within a calendar year.

If your policy deductible is $500, with a hurricane deductible of $4,000, and a hurricane caused damage to your building and/or contents of more than $4,000, you would pay the first $4,000 of the loss, and your insurer would pay the remaining amount. If there were more than one hurricane in the calendar year, and you have already paid the full hurricane deductible due to damages caused by the first hurricane, your deductible for the second and subsequent hurricanes would be the policy deductible. If the damage caused by the first hurricane was less than your hurricane deductible, the deductible and loss payments for the second and subsequent hurricane would be as follows:

	Hurricane #1	Hurricane #2	Subsequent Hurricane
Deductible	$4,000	$1,200	$500
Damage	2,800	3,500	3,000
Insurance Pays	0	2,300	2,500
You Pay	2,800	1,200	500

Since you paid $2,800 of your $4,000 deductible following hurricane #1, the deductible is reduced to $1,200 for hurricane #2. If you changed your insurance company between the first and second hurricane and kept the same hurricane deductible of $4,000, you would pay another $4,000 deductible for the second hurricane because you would lose the deductible credit you had with your previous insurer.

An after effect of a hurricane or major water damage is fungi which include mold or mildew, and spores released into the atmosphere within the house which can affect your health. Due to the very high number of claims following a hurricane, it is very difficult to get repairs done expeditiously as there is usually a shortage of available contractors. As a result, the structure and contents remain damp, which could result in fungi. Most companies limit payment to remove fungi to a maximum of $10,000.

If your home has major damage and it is unsafe or unhealthy to continue living there, you are entitled to additional living expenses until repairs are sufficiently completed so that you can return to your premises, even when minor cosmetic repairs are not finished.

After a hurricane, insurance companies may use their own staff to adjust the hundreds or thousands of additional claims, or the company would probably employ independent adjusters to assist in settling the claims within a reasonable time frame. Although insurers brief independent adjusters on the company's adjusting procedures and policy interpretation, sometimes an independent adjuster may adjust a claim differently than the company's staff adjuster. This may create a problem if you find out that another client, who is also insured by your company received more funds than you did for similar damages. The adjuster is required to give you a copy of the estimate. If you believe you were unfairly treated, or want a detailed explanation regarding the scope of repairs (what will be repaired or replaced), or the settlement calculation, call the adjuster and arrange a meeting to discuss your concerns. For example, some insurers will replace an entire roof if there is one in seven shingles or roof tiles damaged. Removing the damaged shingles or tiles and replacing them is more labour intensive and consequently more expensive than replacing the entire roof or a complete section (slope) of the roof.

If you are still dissatisfied after meeting with your adjuster, call your insurance company and discuss your concerns with a claims supervisor or manager. Quite often, insurers have an on site catastrophe manager located at a temporary office in the affected area who may be able to resolve your concerns immediately. There is also the appraisal process or arbitration.

When all else fails, you can forward a written complaint to either the Federal Emergency Management Agency (FEMA), or your state or provincial Department of Financial Services. Some states have a Commissioner of Insurance, while the provinces each have a Superintendent of Insurance. Insurers have a specified period to respond to complaints made to state or provincial authorities. Usually it is 21 calendar days to respond to the authorities, or 14 days to a claims enquiry from an insured.

CHAPTER 11
Major Claims Process

There are some things that you can do before a major catastrophe which will save a lot of time in the processing of your claim, and perhaps avoid disputes with your insurance company.

1) Locate and check your policy so that you are familiar with your coverage, particularly whether you have Actual Cash Value (ACV) or Replacement Costs (RC) on your building and personal property (contents).

2) Find a safe place to secure your policy and other important documents. You may have a water/fire proof safety box in your home to keep your documents, or you could rent a safety deposit box at your bank.

3) You should always keep a list of expensive items in your home, noting the place and date of purchase, price paid, model and/or serial numbers and purchase documentation (receipts or other proof of purchase as outlined in Chapter 6). You should also take good clear photos, videotape or dvd of the contents in each room in your home. These should be kept at another location in the event there is major damage to your home. It would prevent your proof of purchase/ownership from being completely destroyed.

4) You may be forced to leave your home because of a mandatory emergency evacuation order by the local authorities or due to extensive damage to your home. Prior to the event, you should contact your agent and provide an alternate contact number, perhaps your cell phone. Because electricity may be interrupted for some time following a major catastrophe, internet contact may not be available.

Following a major catastrophe, you should immediately contact your agent to report any damage to your home and personal property. If your company is a direct writer (selling insurance directly to the public instead of through an agent), you should contact the company. Direct writers provide a telephone number to be used to report claims. This number is usually included with the package mailed to you when the policy was originally delivered. To make it convenient for their clients, companies will provide additional ways to report claims. You may be able to report a claim by fax or the internet, and some companies will print a 'Claim Reporting' form in the local newspaper. To report your claim, cut out the form, fill in the information and fax or e-mail it to your company. The fax number and/or e-mail address are printed on the form.

Your policy dictates that you must protect your property from further damage by separating the damaged from the undamaged property. This also speeds up the adjustment process as the adjuster will only have to examine the damaged property. It may not be practical to keep the damaged property due to health concerns. For example, food that is spoilt due to loss of electricity, or carpeting and drapes that cannot be dried quickly which can produce harmful fungi. Be sure to take photos or a video of these items which can be given to your adjuster. It is always a good idea to keep a small sample cut from the carpeting, drapes or fabric covered items before discarding them so that the adjuster will be able to determine the quality. If your home is damaged, prior to your adjuster's visit to document and estimate the damages, you may need to have temporary emergency repairs done to protect the structure and/or contents from further damage. If you are unable to do it yourself, you may have to employ a contractor to board up any open areas until permanent repairs can be made. If you are doing the repairs yourself, keep all receipts of the purchases you made. The contractor should provide you with an invoice detailing the emergency repairs that were done in order to be reimbursed by your insurer.

After a major catastrophe, your insurer may not be able to adjust your claim using a staff adjuster due to the volume of claims reported. Consequently, the adjuster may be from an independent adjusting firm employed by your insurer. Be sure to ask for a business card or some other type of identification. If you are shown some type of identification and you still have concerns, call your insurance company to verify that the individual or firm has been retained by the company as there are multiple scams following a catastrophe.

When the adjuster begins the claims process, it may take one or more visits depending on the severity of the damage and the estimating method used. If he uses an automated property estimating system, he may be able to print the estimate on site during his first visit and provide you with a copy. If the loss is extensive, he may take notes and measurements (called 'scoping' the damage), and prepare the estimate off site, returning sometime later to provide you with a copy. In order to ensure that all the damages are included in the scope or estimate, you should point out to the adjuster on his initial visit, damages that may not be easily apparent which you noticed while doing your own inspection.

Some companies provide checks to their staff adjusters enabling them to pay claims on their initial visit. If you notice damage caused by the event after your claim was paid, you can request another visit by the adjuster to show him the hidden or additional damage that was missed. He will determine if the damage was related to the original cause of loss, and issue a supplementary payment even if you have already signed a final proof of loss.

If there is extensive damage to your personal property (contents of your home), the adjuster will prepare a 'Contents Schedule' (see Chapter 6) listing the damaged contents and indicating which items can be repaired and those that must be replaced. At that stage of the adjustment, your actual cash value or replacement costs policy will determine the amount of your settlement.

If your home is damaged to the extent that you are unable to reside there, you can request an advance payment under your additional living expense coverage. This will provide you with funds to pay for hotel charges, meals and other ongoing expenses. When repairs are completed and you return to your home, the adjuster will calculate what your actual additional expenses were, and pay the final amount after deducting the advance payment(s), (see Chapter 7).

The choice of the contractor to repair your home is made by you. Some insurance companies maintain a list of contractors that have done repairs for their clients for a reasonable price and in a timely and professional manner. However, you are free to select your own contractor or you can use one from the list kept by your insurer. If there is a dispute regarding the cost or scope of the repairs, negotiations should be conducted between the adjuster and contractor. It is not your responsibility to negotiate with the contractor.

You may have two or more contractors bidding on the job. When you are making the choice, be sure to find out if the contractor is from out of state or province. If he is not from the local area, and there are work related issues after the repairs are completed, it may be difficult to locate him or get him to return to the area to correct the problem. You should also determine if he is licensed to work in your state or province by asking to see his license, and check with the local authorities to determine if the license is valid or under suspension. You should also ask to see his liability and workers compensation insurance documents. Read the contract carefully before signing it, and make sure that the materials used are the same quality as listed on the estimate.

Down payments are always a tricky issue. A down payment is usually used to buy the needed materials. You could accompany the contractor when he is buying the materials and pay for it yourself with the funds from your insurer which would eliminate the need for an advance payment. Most reputable contractors have a line of credit with their bank and may not need an advance. If an advance payment is requested, it should not exceed fifty percent of the total estimate. Typically, it should be less. The estimate should show the costs of the materials needed separately from the labour costs. This should show the costs of the materials if there is an advance request. If your insurer gives you a check that is payable jointly to you and your contractor, do not endorse the check and give it to the contractor until the job is completed, and you are satisfied with the quality of the repairs. Before the final payment, ask for a copy of the Release of Lien(s) and/or Certificate of Completion.

Some jurisdictions have laws to prevent gouging. These laws are meant to punish companies or individuals selling food, water, gas, building materials or those offering lodging or storage for an unreasonable price prior to or after a severe weather related or natural event. Some states and provinces have a hot line telephone number so that the public can report price gougers. Price gouging laws are enforced by the Department or Financial Services. Violators are subject to fines, and in cases of multiple violations, possible jail sentences. You should find out in advance the 'gouging hot line' number in the event you may need it.

The information in this book is meant to provide some guidance to the lay person. It covers the most common situations in the claims adjustment process, and attempts to give the reader a basic understanding of the role of the agent, classification of adjusters, policies commonly sold and coverage offered. There are many situations not covered in this book than may apply to the average insured.

You should review your policy to determine the coverage, exclusions, limits and sub-limits. The author has provided examples of coverage limits and sub-limits to illustrate various claims situations. Each claim has a different set of circumstances, and the interpretation of policy wording in each state or province may have changed based on recent court decisions.

Advice, if deemed necessary, should be obtained from qualified professionals in the insurance industry, legal experts or other professionals with specific knowledge of the facts of your claim and the applicable law which would apply in your jurisdiction.

Court cases referenced are not state or province specific, as the purpose of this book is to provide some guidance to the reader in both the United States and Canada.

Glossary of Insurance Terms

Actual Cash Value – Current replacement cost of the item less depreciation.

Additional Living Expenses – The additional cost incurred by you while living at another location when your residence is being repaired.

All Risk Insurance – A policy that covers all perils except those listed as excluded from coverage.

Appraisal – A value placed on property or contents by someone qualified to do so. The insurance contract also has an appraisal procedure when the parties to the contract fail to agree on the costs or scope of repairs or the value of personal property.

Appearance Allowance – If a repair attempt is not 100% successful or the damage is of a minor nature, this is an agreed amount by you and your insurer as a compromise monetary allowance that is paid to you in lieu of any further attempt to repair the damage.

Arbitration – When a dispute between an insured and insurer is heard by an independent person or panel chosen by both parties to resolve the issue in dispute.

Assignment – The transfer of a legal right by you to another party. It cannot be done without the written consent of your insurance company.

Betterments and Improvements – Upgrading done by a condominium unit owner or a tenant. In certain situations the value of the upgrading is not covered by the policy covering the building, but by the unit owner's condo or tenant's policy.

Budget Plan – When premium payments are made to your insurer on a monthly or quarterly basis. Some insurers will charge a small interest charge or a one time fee for the additional paper work. Payments are made via automatic withdrawal from your bank account or on your credit card.

Cite – When an attorney during a legal argument quotes a previous court decision on a similar point of law.

Conditions – Terms and requirements under which the policy is written. It mainly covers issues regarding notice of claim, cancellation and renewal procedures.

Co-Insurance – This provides a financial penalty for not insuring your property for an agreed percentage of the full value, usually 80%. If under insured, you pay a portion of the costs of repairs or replacement.

Consequential Loss – Policies insure against direct loss but sometimes an indirect loss also occurs. For example, loss of frozen food when there is no electricity following a covered cause of loss.

Contingent Fee – An agreement between you and your attorney that fees are paid only if the suit is successful, and payment to the attorney is based on a prior agreed percentage of the award.

Depreciation – Decrease in the value or use life of a structure or item due to age, wear and tear or obsolescence.

Earned Premium – That portion of premium that is non-refundable for the time the company insured the property in the event either party to the contract cancels before the end of the policy period. This is known as a mid term cancellation.

Errors and Omissions Insurance – Professionals are expected to meet the normal standards of their profession. When they fail to do so, this type of policy protects them in the event of an adverse judgment. This policy is also known as E&O insurance.

Estoppel – When the action of your insurance company's representative led you to believe there is coverage for a loss, and you incur an expense based on that belief, the insurer cannot raise coverage issues later in order to avoid paying the claim.

Excess Award – When a court awards a claimant an amount for damages which exceeds the policy limit.

Exclusions – Losses that are not covered and are listed as such.

Financial Interest – In order to place insurance on any property, a person must show that they would suffer a monetary loss if the property was damaged or destroyed.

Friendly Fire – A fire that remains within its confines. For example, a fire in a fireplace, on a stove or BBQ.

Hostile Fire – An uncontrolled fire spreading beyond its confines which causes damage to property.

Insurable Interest – Also called a financial interest.

Liberalization Clause – When a specific policy coverage is broadened, an insurer will immediately extend the broadened coverage to all insureds with similar policies.

Loss Assessment – Condominium owners are sometimes required to pay for repairs to the building even though the building is insured by a separate policy. This assessment may be paid by the unit owners' policy provided the damages are due to a peril that is also covered by the unit owners' policy. The amount payable is subject to a sub-limit. Home owners associations (HOA) may also impose an assessment for debris removal from common areas following a natural disaster.

Loss of Use – Also known as Additional Living Expenses.

Material Change – Any changes to the property or use of the property after it has been insured, that if known to the underwriter, would have made the property no longer acceptable as a risk the insurer would continue to underwrite.

Misrepresentation – The wilful withholding of relevant information which, if known by the underwriter when the application for insurance was accepted, would have made the risk unacceptable or would have required a higher premium.

Mortgage Clause – Insures the mortgagee separately to the extent that a violation of the policy conditions by the insured, does not affect payment to the mortgagee.

Mysterious Disappearance – The failure to locate an item left at a known location within a specific time frame.

Named Peril Insurance – A policy that lists the perils (causes of loss) that are covered by the insurance contract.

Negligence – The failure to act with the same degree of care that an ordinary person would under similar circumstances.

Non Waiver – An agreement after a loss between you and your insurer that would allow the insurer to investigate a loss without creating an estoppel. It does not waive any rights both parties have under the policy.

Pair and Set Clause – Stipulates that the insurer is not obliged to pay for a pair or set, but only for the value of the damaged or lost piece.

Peril – Cause of loss.

Prejudice – When one party's position has been weakened by the actions of another.

Proof of Loss – This document is completed by an insured outlining the circumstances of the loss. It provides enough information which allows the insurer to estimate the value of the loss and in some cases, determine if the loss is covered.

Reservations of Rights – Has the same effect as a Non Waiver. If you refuse to sign a non waiver, this document in the form of a letter is mailed to you.

Risk – The property or item that is the subject of insurance.

Schedule – It lists the items and values insured by the policy. The values are established by written appraisals. Additional premium is charged as it provides broader coverage, and in case of a loss, payments are made for the items in excess of the sub-limits stated in the policy.

Statute – Any law passed by a legislative body empowered to do so.

Statutory Conditions – Requirements in the policy set by law. Statutory conditions are mandatory in some states and provinces.

Subrogation – The insurer's right to recover the amount paid to an insured from a third party that caused the damage or injury.

Tort – A civil wrongful act (as opposed to a criminal activity) which could be accidental or unintentional, resulting in an injury to another party or damage to the property of others.

Unearned premium – That portion of the premium refunded to you if the policy is cancelled prior to the expiration date.

Unoccupied – When the premises is furnished but the occupants are away.

Use Life – The average period of time a consumer can expect a product or property to last before it should be replaced.

Utmost Good Faith – The legal doctrine that requires total honesty by the parties entering into a contract.

Vacant – When the premises is unfurnished and no one resides there.

Valued Schedule – An agreed value of an item listed on a schedule that would be paid in the event of a loss.

Without Prejudice – Renders a previously unaccepted offer made verbally or in writing void, if at a later date the plaintiff attempts to use the offer as evidence of liability.

Karl Hechavarria spent twenty eight years in the claims department of three major United States, Canadian and English property and casualty insurance companies. He has the following designations:

Associate in Claims
Fellow, Chartered Insurance Professional
Associate in Risk Management
Certified Fraud Examiner
Registered Professional Adjuster
Accredited Claims Adjuster (Florida)

Throughout the years, he was a member of multiple claims management associations including the Insurance Institute of Canada, the International Association of Arson Investigators, secretary of the Ontario Chapter of the International Association of Special Investigative Units, past chairman of the Toronto Chapter of IICAR Canada and secretary of the Canadian Automobile Research and Training Association.

He sat on numerous advisory boards and committees dealing with various insurance issues including the Insurance Bureau of Canada, the Ontario Ministry of Transportation, the Insurance Crime Prevention Bureau and the Ontario Collision Reporting Centers. He has given claims related seminars and written multiple in-house papers and programs dealing with catastrophe management and vendor selection process among others.

He currently resides in Florida. He is married and has two sons, a daughter and two step daughters.